Echoes of the Ancient World
Series editor Werner Forman

People of the Totem

People of the Totem

The Indians of the Pacific Northwest

Text by Norman Bancroft-Hunt
Photographs by Werner Forman

Peter Bedrick Books
New York

To the Native people of the Northwest Coast

Page one: Tlingit shaman's healing rattle, depicting a crane with a spirit-shaman on its back
Title page: Totem poles at a Tsimshian village

This edition published in 1989 by
Peter Bedrick Books, New York
© Orbis Publishing Limited, London 1979
All rights reserved. No part of this publication may be reproduced, in any
form or by any means, without the prior written permission of the publisher.
Published by agreement with Macdonald & Co (Publishers) Ltd
Library of Congress Cataloging-in-Publication Data
Bancroft-Hunt, Norman.
People of the totem: the Indians of the Pacific Northwest/text
by Norman Bancroft-Hunt; photographs by Werner Forman.—1st
American ed.
p.   cm.
Bibliography: p.
Includes index.
ISBN 0–87226–199–9
1. Indians of North America—Northwest Coast of North America.
I. Forman, Werner.   II. Title.
E78.N78B36   1989
306′.0899707113—dc19   88–7559
CIP
Printed in Italy
10 9 8 7 6 5 4 3 2 1

Contents

Introduction 7

The Societies 25

The Potlatch 51

The Supernatural 69

Myth and Cosmology 89

Dance and Ceremony 103

Bibliography 126

Acknowledgments 126

Index 126

Introduction

On the Pacific coast of the North American continent, from the mouth of the Columbia River in Washington State through British Columbia and into south-east Alaska as far north as Yakutat Bay, there runs a narrow strip of coastal land and coastal islands geographically isolated from the interior by the mountains of the Coast Range. A cursory glance at this region gives an impression of a harsh environment, alien and hostile to man.

Mountains rise directly from the water's edge and reach snow-capped peaks of a thousand or more metres (three or four thousand feet)—the result of the depression of coastal mountains during the Tertiary and Pleistocene glaciations over ten thousand years ago. These form the major length of the shoreline and extend inland for about a hundred and sixty kilometres (100 miles), preventing any passage except along passes cut by major rivers, notably the Nass, Skeena and Stikine in the north, and the Columbia at the southern boundary.

The ruggedness of the country is emphasized by innumerable inlets and fjords which cut long, narrow and extremely deep channels into the shores, and by a wide off-shore band containing countless islands, which were once the peaks and plateaux of mountains. Some of these are very big—the largest, Vancouver Island, is 32,500 square kilometres

Left : A brooding sky and the sparkle of light reflected from water impart an air of mystery to this typical northern coast landscape.

7

Nearly all the northwest coast archaeological specimens are of stone and have been found in the Fraser River Valley, suggesting that early culture centred in this Coast Salish part of British Columbia.
Above, top: Ceremonial stone dish, probably used as a mortar for grinding tobacco or paint pigment.
Above: Stone effigy head intended to immortalize an important individual.
Left: Transformed by moss, a tree on the Queen Charlotte Islands provides evidence that the area deserves its popular name, 'Rain Coast'.

(12,500 square miles) in area—but many are little more than rocky islets. The measurements of the coast of British Columbia give an idea of the extent of islands and fjords: a straight line from its southern tip around Vancouver up to the Alaskan border measures approximately eight hundred kilometres (five hundred miles), but the actual length of coastline, following all the creeks and inlets, exceeds 27,000 kilometres.

Although the terrain is inhospitable, its severity is tempered somewhat by a mild, wet and windy climate. This is governed by a stream of warm water, known as the Japan Current, which flows north along the edge of the continental shelf at some distance off the coast. Fog banks form along the course of the Current as a result of the warm air it releases, and are driven inshore to blanket the outer coasts. When they change to cloud and rise above the mountains they fall as rain on the inner islands and mainland, producing a very high annual precipitation. The warmth of this air blowing in from the sea governs the coastal temperature, giving cool summers and warm winters. Even in northern localities mid-winter readings are usually above freezing, except on the few days when fierce winds, called williwaws, bring cold air from the interior down the fjords. But, in general, the coastal localities are well-protected by their mountain barrier from the subarctic inland weather conditions.

The Current also displaces cold water, which is forced into the coast. This keeps local water temperature very low and even in the summer months it rises by only two degrees. As this is pushed along the straits, passages and sounds which connect the islands, and through narrow channels leading to wide inlets, it creates fast currents, whirlpools, eddies, rip tides and tidal ranges which may be over 4 metres (14 feet). At times the coast is completely quiet, but storms can quickly create huge waves which batter the shores.

But the dangerous seas are not as deceptive as the land where high canopies of leaves create a dark, dank twilight world inside the forests, even on sunny days, and where the constant sound of dripping water is evidence of the damp which gives rise to a deep carpet of lush, brilliant moss. Moss extends its way up the trunks of the trees and covers everything—solid ground, swamp, rotting vegetation, and smooth stone—making every footfall a potential danger. A person can easily step on what appears to be firm ground, only to hurtle down a rocky slope or to plunge into the depths of a fallen and rotted tree. These fallen trunks present frequent barriers to progress since woods such as cedar decay slowly and may remain for many years.

Trees are mainly coniferous, and grow very tall and thick. Mountainsides are smothered with fir and spruce which commonly stretch from the water's edge almost to the snow line, and there are vast stands of yew, hemlock and cedar. Where the tree cover is thin enough to permit sunlight to penetrate, a tall tangled growth of smaller bushes springs up, particularly around the edges of swamp land and along rivers.

The north Pacific coast presents a forbidding, although undeniably beautiful, aspect. Sometimes thick cloud banks descend to ground level and obscure everything—early ships quite frequently sailed past groups of islands without their crews realizing they were there—but at other times the skies are crystal clear, and snow-capped mountains can be seen glistening in the distance. At these times the sky and sea merge at the horizon at night and, if there is a frost, ice crystals reflect the brilliance of the huge glowing orb of the moon, producing a breathtaking landscape which could well be sprinkled with silver and diamonds.

Even today, with modern equipment and techniques, travel is laborious and time-consuming and communication difficult, confining large populations to the developed areas around communities such as Vancouver, Victoria and Prince Rupert. It was in this region, isolated from any major influence, that the northwest coast Indians, the People of the Totem, developed a civilization which was remarkable in its social customs and cultural achievements.

Exactly when man first arrived on this scene is not known. It is generally accepted that he did not originate in the New World, but came from central Asia during the last Ice-Age, when small groups of Neolithic hunters crossed over an ice-free plain connecting the two continents at the Bering Straits. There were several successive migrations over a long period and some of these people found their way on to the coastal strip when the glaciers began to recede, reaching the Queen Charlotte Islands at least 8000 years ago.

In terms of the type and quantity of natural resources it contained, the area they occupied was eminently suitable for the support of the hunting and gathering communities which they formed : it had an abundance of animal and plant life, and provided plentiful supplies of material for clothing and shelter. However, these were difficult to get at, for the forests were almost impassable and the rivers were often raging torrents deep in vertically sided chasms. Even if a beach was found which could have held a large permanent village, the extraction of timbers to build it seemed insurmountable without sophisticated engineering skills.

We might expect, then, that these fairly rude subsistence cultures would have continued living in the midst of plenty but lacking the ability to use this wealth to advantage. Instead, a sea-dependent culture developed, with navigational skills and seamanship, at least in the local waters, which were superior to those of the European explorers. The people built massive houses from logs and planking, were very advanced in their social organization, art and ceremonial—which included drama and theatre—and were capable of producing the largest wood carvings known to man in the form of totem poles.

The change in their economy began about 4000 years ago—as indicated by the replacement of stone implements, which were unsuitable for sea hunting and fishing, by bone harpoon points. Small more-or-less permanent settlements were established on the sheltered banks of rivers and in coves and bays along the coast, from which ocean-going craft capable of withstanding the dangerous waters of the area were sent out to hunt sea mammals. Since such boats required a considerable ability in working timber, it is logical to assume that the improvement in wood technology happened around this date.

Rows of houses were strung out in a line parallel to the beach where space permitted, but the rugged coastal features dictated that communities were to remain quite small. Therefore, as language groups expanded they split into smaller tribal divisions which were scattered over the region, with the greatest numbers forming in the more hospitable south. Nevertheless, the northwest coast, with some 60–70,000 inhabitants, had one of the highest concentrations of population in aboriginal times, containing about a quarter of the native Americans north of the border with the USA. Some parts, such as the Queen Charlotte Islands and Vancouver Island, supported a larger population than they do today.

When Europeans arrived in the eighteenth century they found the Tlingit Indians occupying the Alaskan panhandle. They were the most northerly of the language groups and had about fifty separate villages which were grouped under fourteen independent tribal divisions. Their territory had previously included areas further to the south, but they had been forced out of these by the expansion of their southern neighbours, the Tsimshian, who now had nine tribes living on former Tlingit lands around Prince Rupert. Another five Tsimshian tribes lived along the coast as far south as Milbanke Sound and maintained close contact with their Prince Rupert relatives who were part of the same dialect division. Speakers of two other Tsimshian dialects, the Niska on the Nass River and the Gitskan on the Skeena River, extended their villages for some distance inland where they controlled much of the traffic along these river routes to the interior.

Adjacent to the Tlingit and Tsimshian, on the Queen Charlotte Islands, were the Haida. They were feared by many other coast people because of their daring war exploits, and had a reputation for undertaking long, perilous sea voyages. They were a very distinct group, although their language was related to that of the Tlingit, with numerous loosely organized villages which were frequently little more than large extended families. A few Haida separated from the main body during the middle of the eighteenth century and took up residence on Prince of Wales Island in Alaska, where they are referred to as the Kaigani-Haida.

On the mainland, the southern neighbours of the Tsimshian were members of the Kwakiutl language group, speaking the Heiltsuk, or Bella Bella, dialect. A few Kwakiutl lived further north, inland of the Tsimshian, and a southern dialect was spoken on the coast between Rivers Inlet and Knight Inlet, and along the northern shores of Vancouver Island. All told, the language was spoken by some twenty-five autonomous tribal groups living in different villages and without a cohesive cultural identity.

They shared Vancouver Island with Salish- and Nootkan-speaking peoples. The coastal division of the Salish lived along the Strait of Georgia coast and on the adjacent mainland around Puget Sound, with other groups in the western portion of Washington State, where they kept in trade contact with interior people who spoke a related language. Their social organization was as scattered family groups, and consequently there were many very small communities spread over a large area. An isolated enclave of Coast Salish, the Bella Coola, lived further north on the mainland in the Kwakiutl area and had adopted a culture which was almost identical with that of their neighbours.

Right : Although highly stylized, northwest coast design was often extremely functional. Since they were intended as trade items, bentwood boxes were frequently painted with designs which could be identified with several different crest animals. The sides of this box, which is probably Haida, have been made by grooving, steaming and bending a single plank of red cedar.

Below : The horns and cloven hoofs of a mountain goat are readily recognized on this Haida spruce root hat, which was worn as a symbol of its owner's clan affiliation. The goat is not native to the Queen Charlotte Islands and the crest was probably obtained through trade with the Tsimshian.

Far right, above : Slots on this Bella Coola stone pile-driver form an integral part of the composition but were designed to support the user's thumbs, giving a better grip when the implement was used for pounding.

Far right, below : Californian abalone shell was a major trade item since the local variety was thin and pallid. It was extensively used for inlay work. The Kwakiutl fashioned the shells into plaques, known as 'Twenty-Dollar size' from their value in 1900. The perforation in this example suggests that it was worn as an ornament.

About twenty Nootkan tribes lived on Vancouver's Pacific coast, with small local groups in their central and southern divisions, but stronger confederated tribal units in the north. A Nootkan dialect was also spoken on the other side of Juan de Fuca Strait, at Cape Flattery, by the Makah. Linguistically, these groups were linked with the Kwakiutl, but they had no feelings of solidarity with them and did not consider themselves relatives.

Not only were these people spread out in a number of language and dialect divisions, but they were also quite different in physical appearance. Those to the north, the Tlingit, Tsimshian and Haida, were much taller than the Kwakiutl and Nootka. Salish stature was similar to that of the Kwakiutl, but they were markedly darker in skin coloration than any other of the northwest coast Indians. However, although their early history is poorly documented, we know that they were all of Mongolian stock. In fact, the Tlingit, Haida, and interior Athabascans resemble the Palaeo-Siberian Chukchee, Koryak and Yukaghir so closely that they are sometimes classified together as one physical type.

Split-representation, an art form which characteristically separates the subject into a number of elements which are recombined according to regularized rules, appears in the art of these prehistoric Siberians and among the tribes of the northwest coast, and, according to the French anthropologist Levi-Strauss, among the Caduveo—the remnants of the once flourishing Guaicuru nation of Brazil—the Maori of New Zealand, and the archaic Chinese. Franz Boas describes this art, with reference to the northwest coast, as 'two profiles which adjoin at mouth and nose . . . either the animals are represented as split in two so that the profiles are joined in the middle, or a front view of the head is shown with two adjoining profiles of the body' (Boas *Primitive Art* pp. 223–4).

Northwest coast cultural traditions show almost unbroken continuity prior to the arrival of Europeans. The few minor culture changes are the result of limited borrowings from other people. The Tlingit and Tsimshian used some skin clothing (it was generally made from beaten cedar bark) and porcupine quill decoration as a result of trade contacts with the interior Athabascans. Along the central coast the impassable mountains prevented almost all outside contact, but there were vast trade networks in the south, where environmental and cultural conditions were most similar.

The Chinook tribes acted as middlemen between the southern northwest coast and other groups at the Dalles—a large inter-tribal trade area on the Columbia River—where skins, dried salmon, fish oil and other similar commodities were exchanged for items such as Californian abalone shell. These were then traded by the southern tribes along the length of the coast.

The extent of this trade is apparent in the journeys made by some of the northern Tlingit, who travelled by canoe over distances of 1600 kilometres (1000 miles) to obtain goods from the tribes living around Puget Sound. Both the Haida and Tsimshian manufactured cedar wood boxes purely for trading purposes which bore designs in the split-representational style of animal crests but did not represent any particular animal species. This meant that they could be purchased by other groups and did not have to be identified with the symbols used by specific families.

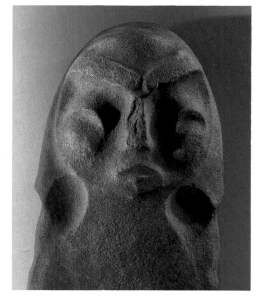

Goods were also introduced from other areas and many items of material culture may be traced back to China, including wood slat armour, forms of woven hats and grave-markers, and some types of edged club. Certainly some are attributable to fairly recent cultural exchange or are due to the influence of early Russian traders who operated in Tlingit territory and introduced Chinese goods prior to the arrival of the European explorers. Some leather articles from the northern tribes are embossed with ancient Chinese coins and large blue Russian beads were popularly used items. The Russians remained until 1867 when they sold Alaska to the United States.

European attention was first focused on the area in the search for the Northwest Passage which supposedly connected the Atlantic and Pacific Oceans. Rumours of ships having sailed in these regions, and inventive letters and ships' logs documenting the voyages excited the imaginations of scientists, politicians and businessmen. Many of them staked their reputations and, less frequently, their fortunes on proving the existence of this short route to China. But it was not until 1774, when the Spaniard Juan Perez sailed from Mexico to the Queen Charlottes (where he was too timid to make landfall) that European contact was made with the Indians.

Perez traded at Vancouver Island with the curious Nootkans who boarded his ships, and two more Spanish vessels visited the coast in the following year. Then, three years later, the English ships *Resolution* and *Discovery* arrived under the command of Captain James Cook.

He anchored his ships in Nootka Sound, on Vancouver Island, for nearly a month while they were refitted, and during this time he kept a journal of his discoveries and relationship with the Nootkan Indians he met. The native attitudes he recorded were quite typical of these coastal people, and, together with notes kept by some of his officers, are invaluable sources of information about aboriginal culture.

Upon arrival he was met by canoes whose crews, according to Second Lieutenant King:

'perform'd what seemed a necessary ceremony, which was pulling & making a circuit round both Ships with great swiftness, & their

Paddles kept in exact time; one man would stand up in the middle with a Spear or rattle in his hand, & a mask on which was sometimes the figure of a human face, at others that of an Animal, & kept repeating something in a loud tone. At other times they would all join in a Song, that was frequently very Agreeable to the Ear, after this they always came alongside & began to trade without Ceremony.' (King's *Journal*, 1 April 1778.)

It might be added that Cook was so pleased with his reception that he ordered the ship's company to serenade the Indians with the fife and drum, and then with french horns. King noted that: 'These were the only people we had seen that ever paid the smallest attention to those or any of our musical Instruments.'

The intensive pattern of aboriginal trade was to govern Cook's dealings with the Indians throughout his visit, and he noticed that they extended this to include goods which natives he had met in other parts of the world did not consider as trade items. They had a well-defined sense of ownership and tribal boundaries, so that when Cook wished to cut some grass for his animals he was suddenly confronted

Right: Although this carved wooden bowl is said to represent a seal, the presence of the tail and paws make it almost certain that a sea-otter is really depicted. It has an interesting design concept in which the animal's form takes precedence: the entire carving is an animal which happens to contain a bowl, and is not a bowl shape with added appendages. The eye form used to indicate the shoulder joint is a common northwest coast design element, but the style of the carving is typically Kwakiutl.
Far right: Trade patterns meant that artifacts were scattered along the length of the coast. This human face mask was collected among the Haida in 1879 and subsequently attributed to the Tsimshian, but is probably of Nootkan manufacture. Much of its visual strength is due to the bold, simple, geometric decoration and the restricted modelling of the features which, in profile, form one line through the forehead and nose and then recede abruptly to a small mouth and chin—characteristics of Nootkan carving.

by almost the entire tribe demanding payment for this service. He realized that he would not have been so presumptuous in Europe and agreed to pay for this privilege. When they were cutting wood at a later date his crew ignored the demands, and, although the Indians did not stop them, they made a point of continually reminding Cook that they had only allowed them to continue because they were friends.

He found that they had a well-organized system of discussing prices among the entire group before making an agreement and that the values of their goods increased if the purchaser seemed prepared to pay more. They were completely trustworthy with the exception of an irresistible urge to obtain metals which made it necessary to guard his boats so that they would not be stripped of metal parts. Even then, 'One fellow would amuse the boat keeper at one end of the boat while another was pulling her to pieces at the other.'

Nevertheless, he was so impressed by their friendly disposition and general honesty that, at his departure, as a token of his regard, he gave a present to an Indian he knew well. He received a valuable beaver skin in return and made a further gift to match its worth; but the Indian took off his beaver cloak, which Cook knew he valued highly, and

insisted that the Captain accept it. Moved at this generosity, Cook made a presentation of his personal sabre with a copper handle; whereupon he was urged to return so that he could be given many furs.

Cook's voyage, more than any other, was responsible for the influx of European traders who were to cause tremendous upheaval in the Indian cultures. He noted in his journal that:

'A great many canoes filled with the Natives were about the Ships all day, and a trade commenced betwixt us and them, which was carried on with the Strictest honisty on boath sides. Their articles were the Skins of various animals, such as Bears, Wolfs, Foxes, Dear, Rackoons, Polecats, Martins and in particular the Sea Beaver [sea otter] . . . For these things they took in exchange, Knives, chissels, pieces of iron and Tin, Nails, Buttons, or any kind of metal. Beads they were not fond of and cloth of all kinds they rejected.' (Cook's *Journal*, 30 March 1778.)

Midshipman Edward Riou endorsed Cook's comments on trading:

'The Natives continue their Visits bringing with them apparently every thing they are in possession of, but nothing is so well received by us as skins, particularly those of the sea beaver or Otter, the fur of which is very soft and delicate.' (Riou's *Journal*, 1 April 1778.)

Both accounts lay special emphasis on the sea otter, and when the ships called at Canton in China on their return voyage to England these furs were sold for fantastic prices. The news was published in Europe in 1785, although Cook was not responsible since he had been killed in Hawaii, and thus began the northwest coast and China fur trade which was to bring dozens of ships of all nationalities to the coast during the following twenty-five years. An example of the value of this trade is given by the British captain Dixon who, in 1788, spent a month on the coast purchasing furs which he was able to sell in China for ninety thousand pounds.

As far as Indian culture was concerned, the main effect of the European ships was to increase the extent of aboriginal trade patterns, since tribes in contact with whites would purchase furs from more remote groups in order to supplement their stocks. The ships' captains, however, were interested only in remaining long enough to load their cargoes and set off again quickly in their search for high profits. They had no desires to convert or influence the 'heathens' in any way; therefore, no drastic changes occurred in the Indian way of life during this early trade.

The sea otter was hunted to such a degree by the end of the second decade of the nineteenth century that trading in these furs was no longer viable. Nevertheless, the area had been opened up to exploitation, and enough interest in other furs had been generated for the North West and Hudson's Bay Companies to see fit to establish a series of trading posts between 1800 and 1850.

With the ready availability of trade goods, native institutions based on wealth were able to develop to a hitherto impossible degree. An important feature of Indian life was a ceremonial known as the potlatch. This was used to validate social rank by a claimant to a position of privilege demonstrating that he had sufficient wealth to maintain the position. Manufacturing items (wealth goods) by traditional processes was a slow and laborious task, which limited the goods available within the community. However, purchasing them from a store was an entirely different prospect since it depended only on having enough furs to do so, and the Indians were past masters at using these trade opportunities to their advantage. There was consequently a rapid increase in the personal wealth of individuals and families, and potlatch ceremonies became larger and more frequent.

Left : This humanoid Bella Coola mask, which may represent an ancestor, shows the Bella Coola predilection for painting across curved surfaces in the carving. The light areas are negative aspects of the design, created by the positive 'U' forms which suggest facial painting.
Above : There was a large influx of Chinese on the northern part of the coast in the 1870s and 1880s, particularly around the Tlingit village of Sitka, when European-owned salmon canneries drafted in a Chinese workforce to replace seasonal Indian labour. This caused considerable tension and the Tlingit only permitted the Chinese to land on condition that they undertook to return to China after training. In this carving a Tlingit artist has successfully captured the features and dress of one of these immigrant workers.

Many traditional activities continued in this basically unchanged but very much exaggerated form. Economic life still relied on native methods of hunting, but had the added impetus of accumulating vast surpluses for trading and for use at ceremonial feasts. The increased importance of feasts required greater amounts of ceremonial paraphernalia in the form of woodcarvings, costumes, masks, blankets and so on; thus, the artists were busier and produced more, using iron chisels obtained in exchange for their furs.

Naturally, the traders encouraged this growth, since it served their own interests, and tribes began to move into the areas surrounding the posts so that they would have trade advantages. As a result traditional enemies found themselves on lands very close to one another. This introduced a competitive element in potlatching which therefore required ever-increasing amounts of wealth, and changed its form very drastically so that it began to bear little resemblance to the traditional ceremony.

Much of the wealth was obtained through normal trading methods, yet there were other means of raising money for the purchase of potlatch goods by providing services for which the whites were only too eager to pay large sums. Prostitution of Indian women at logging camps, white population centres and to the crews of trading ships, became an important and honourable way of earning income for status-seeking ventures. This trade developed only because of the demands made by whites and owed nothing to native custom. Among the Indians themselves chastity was a highly valued quality, and prostitution virtually unknown. In fact, a woman who flaunted her favours would be regarded as 'crazy'.

A consequence of prostitution was the introduction of venereal diseases which seriously affected the child-bearing abilities of Indian women. Since mothers, wives and daughters might stay for some time at the logging camps, entire families were infected, and this also exposed them to other European diseases against which they had no resistance. Smallpox, measles and influenza, plus the effects of adulterated whisky used as a trade item, were to reduce the Indian population by nearly two thirds before the end of the 1800s. The Haida, in less than a hundred years, decreased in number from about 8000 to under 500; and in just one smallpox outbreak which began in Victoria in 1862, almost a third of the total population died, in spite of Governor Douglas's attempts to seal the city.

When missionaries began seeking converts they met with tribes who were already in a state of decline, their numbers decimated and their culture disrupted. In some areas a complete generation had lost the traditional skills and become dependent on trade goods. Although the priests began to take a serious interest in the moral welfare of the native inhabitants in 1849, when Vancouver Island was colonized in confirmation of British sovereignty and Victoria became a centre for their activities, they did not reach many of the tribes until the late nineteenth century. By this time most of them had been visited by Indian prophets who had picked up some concepts of Christianity during their travels. This, together with the damage caused to their societies, made the Indians more inclined to accept white preaching than they might otherwise have been. Even so, many of the first mission attempts were failures since there was little reason for the adoption of a religion which was inferior, in terms of local tradition and environment, to that already in use, and which was obviously not being practised by the whites themselves—early missionaries travelled on trading ships whose crews were hardly paragons of Christian virtue! The establishment of churches was further hindered by rivalry between various religious factions, since the priests argued bitterly among themselves as to who had the right to bestow the blessing of Christian charity on the 'savages'.

With the exception of a few groups who set up model Christian villages with a priest at their head, tacit opposition was fairly widespread,

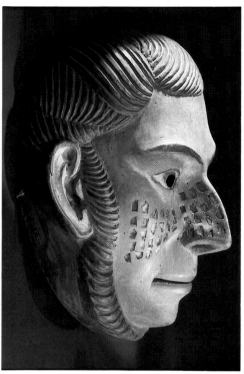

Above, top : A Tlingit stone pipe, representing a whale chasing a seal, using a circular composition to create the illusion of motion. The whale's head contains the pipe bowl; the mouthpiece is between the seal's head and whale's tail. Tobacco cultivated prior to European contact was chewed rather than smoked.
Above : The characteristic face shape, features and freckles of a European show that Haida artists were capable of realistic portraiture.
Above, right : The meanings of the numerous coast petroglyphs (rock-carvings) are often unclear. They may have been boundary markers, records of important events, or magical symbols. These are located at the outlet of Sproat Lake near Port Alberni in Nootkan territory.

although it was not so much against Christian ideals but was directed at the fact that embracing these meant giving up native customs. The missionary, it must be remembered, was the most Victorian example of middle-class virtue to which the Indian had been exposed and he usually condemned any customs which were outside his own frame of reference. He was disgusted by the near-nudity of the 'heathens' and insisted they wore European clothing. What he saw as a total lack of morals horrified him, even though sexual licence within the tribes was not overtly permissive and in many instances, as for example during the period of a girl's puberty, was extremely strict.

The prevalence of prostitution tended to confirm his beliefs, so he vented his anger on the natives, without making much attempt to understand the reasons or to censure the white communities where it originated and which encouraged its continuance. Missionaries tried to prevent occasions which they erroneously thought afforded an opportunity for illicit sexual activity, namely, the large ceremonial dance meetings. Eventually legislation was passed which outlawed many of the traditional cultural activities, which, nevertheless, continued to be practised in secret in somewhat changed forms.

This legislation formed part of the Indian Act of the 1880s, a document which assumed that the Indian population would decline rapidly and which sought a solution for what it regarded as the 'Indian problem'. The 'problem', of course, was that the indigenous peoples were thought culturally and morally inferior, and therefore had to be subjected to a policy designed in their best interests by a white administration, until such time as they should cease to exist as a culturally different unit and either vanish or merge imperceptibly into white society. Indian affairs were, in effect, to be taken out of the control of the Indians.

Before this could be implemented, the people it was directed at had to be confined within certain areas where their 'progress' and 'welfare' might be supervised. To this end the village sites of local bands were set aside as reserves, most of which were established without recourse to treaty agreements. Only fourteen treaties were actually made, with a few tribes on Vancouver Island. These were due to the beneficence of Governor Douglas since the land had become Crown property when it was colonized and there was no legal obligation on him to purchase it. Elsewhere aboriginal title was either disclaimed or ignored: the government simply allowed free settlement of lands outside areas designated as reserves. Since the Indians were fishermen anyway, there was little opposition from them to these claims.

Opposition did, however, arise to the Indian Agents, who were local government superintendents, charged with the task of administering funds and ensuring that government policy was carried out effectively. Some of them were knowledgeable men with a genuine sympathy for the Indians, but many were ignorant and interested only in lining their own pockets from government funds. Sadly, the opinions of the latter carried most weight, and their annual reports were largely responsible for vast sums of money being spent on the intensification of an agricultural programme, in a country where agricultural development is decidedly limited even today. Educational policy directed that Indian children were the charge of the church and that they should attend a mission school.

Schools often procured their pupils by forcibly removing them from their families and based education on the principle that the Indian was inferior. Children were forbidden to speak their own language even among themselves, with a severe beating meted out as punishment if they infringed this rule. By the time they completed their schooling they found it difficult to fit into Indian society, which demanded a traditional upbringing and strict adherence to forms of social etiquette. As white society still regarded them as 'savage', they were rejected by the very group whose ideals they had been forced to encompass. Although welcomed back by their own communities, they experienced a conflict within themselves which resulted in a crisis of identity; thus, the beginning of the twentieth century, by which time the schools were thoroughly established, saw a rapid degeneration in native cultures.

Another effect of the Indian Act was its attempt to limit native movement by requiring Indians to register their names with the Agent controlling the reserve. Nominally this was so that they would be eligible for government aid, tax exemption, etc. But a registered Indian was not necessarily Indian by birth. Children born to an Indian father were automatically granted Indian status; an Indian woman who married a white man lost this, as did any of her children below the age of majority. The children resulting from the marriage were classed as white. Conversely, a white woman and her children gained status through marriage to an Indian. Thus, the anomalous situation developed where a full-blooded Indian could be classified as white if his mother had remarried while he was very young. This principle caused, and still causes, very deep resentment among the Indian communities.

At the end of the nineteenth and beginning of the twentieth centuries, then, the northwest coast was undergoing a major adjustment to a totally new set of social conditions in which traditional values had been severely undermined, but where no new ones had offered an adequate

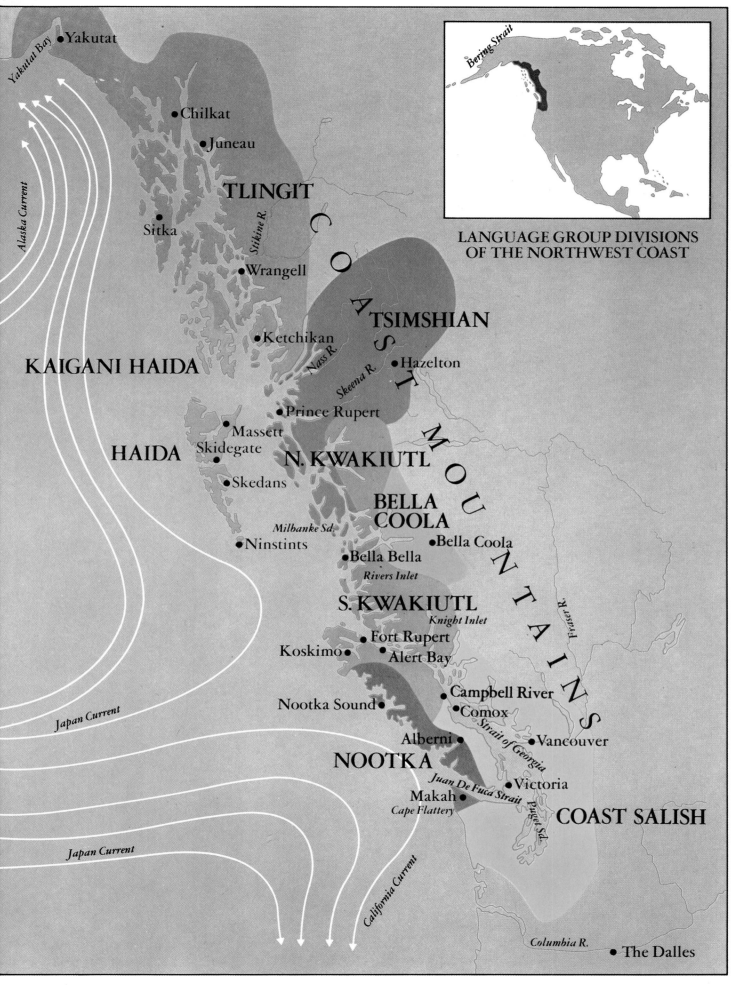

LANGUAGE GROUP DIVISIONS
OF THE NORTHWEST COAST

Bering Strait

Yakutat Bay
●Yakutat

Alaska Current

●Chilkat

●Juneau

TLINGIT

Stikine R.

Sitka●

●Wrangell

C O A S T

TSIMSHIAN

●Ketchikan

Nass R.

KAIGANI HAIDA

Skeena R. ●Hazelton

●Prince Rupert

●Massett

Skidegate●

HAIDA

N. KWAKIUTL

M O U N T A I N S

●Skedans

Milbanke Sd.

BELLA
COOLA

●Ninstints

●Bella Coola

Bella Bella●

Rivers Inlet

S. KWAKIUTL

Knight Inlet

Japan Current

●Fort Rupert

Fraser R.

Koskimo● ●Alert Bay

●Campbell River

Nootka Sound● ●Comox

Japan Current

●Alberni

Strait of Georgia

●Vancouver

NOOTKA

Juan De Fuca Strait

Makah● ●Victoria

Cape Flattery

Puget Sd.

COAST SALISH

California Current

Columbia R.

●The Dalles

21

substitute. Many native people took employment with white logging concerns, where they found the system of work incentives which offered a man extra money to stay away from home for several months to be unintelligible. Indian families are very close and as long as one member had food and shelter to offer there was no reason for any member to be absent. Fishing was more to his liking, since this was seasonal work and was a continuation of the aboriginal economic pattern, but this created problems in accepting authority. Indian life was based on communal sharing, and, as it was quite common for the Indian to know more about fish than his skipper, he saw no reason for accepting the indignity of bowing to this man's demands.

There was also his different attitude towards money and goods. Indian society did not value material goods in the same way as white society. The Indian's only reason in accumulating wealth was the status it gave him when he distributed it in establishing a claim to a social position. When this had been established then the stimulus to work was removed and he preferred to spend his time with his family or in social and ceremonial engagements, rather than accumulate further wealth in long periods of employment.

The solution was to claim independence and become self-employed. To this end the Indians found an ally in the canning industry which rented boats, or lent money to purchase them, and wrote up contracts to take the catches from Indian fishermen. This left the Indians free to operate their fishing fleets on a co-operative basis. Since the fishing and ceremonial seasons coincided with the seasons in which these activities traditionally took place, this satisfied the demands of seasonal work and permitted the observation of the ceremonies. It also enabled families to remain united.

After 1930 the population began to increase and the problems of administration suddenly changed. Native numbers were growing at a faster pace than those of the whites; the Indian was regaining his confidence and asserting himself once more; he was demanding independence; and furthermore he was using his knowledge of white societies to fight back at them through their own legal processes. An uneasy situation developed in which adjoining white and Indian communities barely tolerated each other's proximity, and where there was an atmosphere of deeply rooted suspicion on both sides.

Indians once again felt proud of their race and strove to piece together the fragments of their societies, although they also realized that the traditional ways of life could never be fully regained. Many schools are now run by the Indians themselves using their own languages as vital parts of the curriculum; young people are expressing an interest in traditional dances and social organization and are turning for instruction to those few older members of the tribes with knowledge of the past. The bands—since reserves are not always complete tribal units—have been more vociferous in their demands for recognition of their rights to fishing areas and resources, presenting their claims through band councils which often contain highly erudite and capable members. Although claims have tended to be dealt with on a local band basis, there are organizations, such as the Union of British Columbia Chiefs, the Native Brotherhood, and the British Columbia Homemakers (a women's pressure group), which are pressing matters of general concern as a larger, and therefore more powerful, body.

Government agencies have been making genuine efforts to improve relationships with the Indian communities and a number of courts have ruled favourably in cases of native rights. Unfortunately, the louder voices of business lobbyists and industry frequently overshadow the demands and protests of the Indian minority, and the lack of treaties means that aboriginal title to lands must be established before any settlements can be considered. From the Indian point of view these lands have never been ceded and white communities are in effect squatting on native property. Nevertheless, many adjacent native–white townships have started working on a co-operative basis in which they share amenities and solve problems together—but others are still very separate.

Such, then, is the situation today. It remains to be seen what the outcome of this revivalism will be since native culture is still in a state of flux. But they are far from being the vanishing race they were once thought to be.

Nearly all the extant artifacts date from the nineteenth century. Earlier examples have decayed since they were mainly made from wood and very few have been made during the twentieth century (excepting very recent examples of masks and so on, and those made for the tourist trade). From the 1800s we also have the first-hand accounts of native customs made by observers before white influences caused many changes. It is this period which accordingly gives us the best picture of the culture and society of the northwest coast Indians.

Below : View to the north of Skedans village on the Queen Charlotte Islands. Skedans was renowned as a peaceful town which did not have the traditions of warring common to its neighbouring Haida villages. Introduced diseases decimated the population and the narrow isthmus on which this once flourishing village stood was deserted about a century ago.

The Societies

Left: Prow ornaments were mounted on the large Tlingit war canoes as formal symbols of importance. This carving of an owl with outstretched wings was one of the crests used by the Raven division at Klukwan, the largest of the Chilkat Tlingit villages. It must have presented an awesome spectacle when perched on the high, projecting prow of an 18 m. (60 ft) canoe, and is itself 1.2 to 1.3 m. high (4ft to 4ft 6in.). It is beautifully carved and painted, inlaid with abalone shell and trimmed with the fur of a brown bear.

When the first European explorers sailed along the northwest coast they were met by Indians in canoes. Captain Cook and his crew assumed that the Nootkan Indians they met spent more time in these than on land, causing Second Lieutenant James King, on board the *Resolution*, to describe them as 'loose & ill shap'd particularly about the Knees & legs, owing as we suppose to their being much in their Canoes, & sitting upon their heels' (King's *Journal* 'Notes on the Description of the Inhabitants').

It may be that he was given this impression simply because the novelty of their visit had made the Indians stop their normal activities and paddle out to the English ships out of curiosity and to trade. In fact, a number of them spent entire nights sleeping in their boats beside the *Resolution* and *Discovery*. But he was correct in realizing that they depended on sea and river transport and had an extensive knowledge of the local waters, and this was true of all these coastal people. The Haida on the Queen Charlottes, whose waters are renowned for their fierceness and unpredictability, were 'especially skilful in the management of their well-built canoes' according to the missionary Charles Harrison, who had the opportunity to observe more of the Indians' normal life than Cook.

Any village had numbers of boats drawn up on the beach in front of the houses. Many were small utility craft, used mainly by the women for off-shore fishing and for local visiting, and there were always some

specialized sealing-canoes which were raised up on log platforms to prevent any damage being caused to their highly polished hulls. These were streamlined and had been carefully burnished so that they would make no sound as they knifed through the water. A few eighteen-metre (sixty-foot) ceremonial canoes, with painted sides and huge prow or stern sections, would be covered with protective layers of cedar bark matting and be lying beside some of the houses.

Making a canoe was a long, arduous task. A suitable section of tree trunk had to be split out using wooden wedges, and this was then hollowed and roughly shaped by a combination of adzing and burning before final shaping could begin. This last stage involved filling the hollowed-out section with water and dropping in red-hot stones, so that the boiling water would make the wood pliable enough to be forced into its final form when thwarts were hammered into position. Many of the larger and specialized types were made by craftsmen, but every man was capable of producing a serviceable utility boat.

Villages were sited with careful reference to beaches, since the sealing-canoes had to be carried above high water mark (they were never dragged for fear of damaging the polish), with a narrow, steeply sloping sand or gravel beach being preferred. They were in sheltered locations, usually small bays, which offered protection from sudden violent storms. The approach was from the sea and the first impression was of the mass of totem poles which fronted the houses, some of which served as house posts in that they supported heavy logs which formed the main roof beams. Over the main log framework of the building there were a number of smaller poles covered with cedar bark planks, split and adzed in a manner similar to that employed in canoe-making, forming a massive, multi-family dwelling up to fifty metres (one hundred and sixty feet) long and twelve metres (forty feet) wide. They were known as a 'Long-House' to the Salish groups but called 'Big-House' elsewhere along the coast.

Since they served both for habitation and as ceremonial buildings during winter for staging large feasts, the leading houses of the village were bigger and more impressive than the others. Sometimes the planking was whitewashed with lime and then covered with a magnificent painted symbol of, say, the Killer Whale or Beaver to denote the owner's lineage. Kwakiutl houses often had the entire front painted in this manner, while some of the northern groups restricted the painting to around the doorway. The brilliance of the blacks, reds, and blue-greens used in painting caused Spanish and French chroniclers to gasp in admiration when they saw them set against the wooded mountains directly behind the village, for they lent a majesty to buildings which were already impressive because of their size.

Carvings stood in front of the house, at the top of the beach, as well as being used as supports for these buildings (the Salish sometimes had carved figures standing along each side of their Long-Houses), to frame the doorways or occasionally to form the actual entrance. The presence of these three-dimensional forms was emphasized by the flat painting behind them and by the pattern of the wide cedar planking, making them a powerful assertion of the family's position in the tribe.

Planking on the side of the house was secured in place by thongs, or with antler or wood pegs, but the roof boards were left loose. A valuable authority here is John Jewitt, a Boston seaman who was captured by the Nootka after their chief, Maquinna, had ordered the massacre of the crew of his ship as a reprisal for the atrocities of earlier traders. He was kept as a slave for three years but was well-treated in return for his services as a blacksmith, and came to admire their skill in building, of which he left this vivid description:

'the top is covered with planks of eight feet broad, which form a kind of coving projecting so far over the ends of the planks that form the roof, as completely to exclude the rain. On these they lay large stones to prevent their being displaced by the wind. The ends of the planks are not secured to the beams on which they are laid by any fastening, so that in a high storm, I have often known all the men obliged to turn out and go upon the roof to prevent them from being blown off, carrying large stones and pieces of rock with them to secure the boards; always stripping themselves naked on these occasions, whatever may be the severity of the weather, to prevent their garments from being wet and muddied, as these storms are almost always accompanied with heavy rains . . . [The houses] are wholly without a chimney, nor is there any opening left in the roof, but whenever a fire is made, the plank immediately over it is thrust aside, by means of a pole, to give vent to the smoke.' (*Narrative of the Adventures and Suffering of John R. Jewitt* pp. 69–70.)

His reference to moving a plank above the fire refers to the Nootkan practice of having separate fireplaces in front of each family's space, on a raised platform around the sides of the house. Some of the other groups used only one central fireplace, therefore moving the central planks adjoining the ridge-pole, and sometimes the sleeping areas were partitioned off with screens or with piles of boxes. Interior details varied, but there were always spaces allocated according to social position with the most important family at the rear, away from the entrance.

It was necessary to bend double to pass through the small door-opening and enter a single large, gloomy and smoke-filled room which in some groups was excavated to a depth of about a metre. The only light was admitted through the spaces opened in the roof and from the glow of the fires, but it was much brighter during fine weather, when most of the side planks were removed. However, the wet and windy climate must have dictated that these were generally firmly secured.

Among the northern groups, this room was dominated by a plank screen which had a small oval opening cut through its centre and was painted with an image similar to those on the outsides of some houses. The screen was framed by two carved and painted posts supporting double ridge-poles, and divided the house into a communal living area, in front of the screen, and a religious area, behind it. This part acted as storage for the boxes containing ceremonial paraphernalia, which could only be used by members of their secret societies.

These northern homes were overburdened with a profusion of carved images and in addition to the screen and posts there were numerous decorated articles which littered the rooms. The most common article of furniture was the cedar chest—they were used for storing possessions and as containers for dried foods. Further decoration included carved friezes on the raised platforms, and the ridge-pole, which was carved and painted. The Kwakiutl laid greater emphasis on elaborate painting, and Kwakiutl groups had carved and painted cedar settees for the use

House posts and screens were frequently carved and painted with images relating to mythological tales. One such tale was that of Bear-mother. In this, a young woman was taken to the home of the Bears as a punishment for insulting them; she married the Bear-chief's son and gave birth to two semi-human cubs. Although this tale originated among the Tsimshian, it spread from there to other language groups.

Far left: The two human faces of the children of Bear-mother are clearly seen on the palms of this carved housepost, 1.9m (6ft 3in) high. It portrays a bear in a squatting position. The post once supported the roof beam of a northern Kwakiutl house in the village of Kitimaat.

Left: A painted Tlingit version of the squatting bear on a 4.5m (15ft) high 'Nahen', or house partition screen. An oval opening at the base of this screen provided access to the sacred room at the rear of Chief Shakes' house at Wrangell. The bear shown is the Brown Bear clan crest of Chief Shakes and is a magnificent example of two-dimensional Tlingit art.

of the ruling families. All groups had a varied assortment of small objects such as spoons, bowls and cradles.

Apart from these, the house also contained stores of food which had been baled up and were kept above the sleeping spaces or among the rafters; bladder bags, packed with fish oil, were suspended from the roof, together with racks on which fish had been left to smoke-dry. Blankets and furs served as clothing and bedding, and the materials being used in the pursuit of various crafts—strips of cedar bark, lengths of mountain goat wool and dog hair, bundles of sea-lion whiskers— were piled up wherever someone was busy at work.

People squatted around the fires, and sat or lay on the platforms in order to keep below the level of the smoke. Naturally there was constant commotion as they went about their various activities, but most of their spare time, particularly in the evenings, would be spent in or around the house exchanging stories and discussing day-to-day affairs, or gambling. The Nootka held laughing competitions, in which two teams sat and stared straight-faced at each other while bets were placed as to which would break into a smile first. They prove that the European's impression of the Indian as a stoic was a false one, although it is true that he went to great lengths to avoid showing his emotions in front of strangers. Most gambling was a variation on the bone game which used marked sticks and dice (it was also known in the plains and prairies and among the Eskimo), and was accompanied by special gambling songs and drumming, with frequent shouts of jubilation.

These amusements were more common in the winter when inclement weather kept people indoors, and served to while away the long evenings between other social engagements. It was at this time of year also that the major villages were continuously occupied and ceremonies took place. As centres of ceremonial activity houses had ritual significance and were given sacred names. It was really the house site rather than the building that was sacred, and so buildings could be extended, rebuilt, or enlarged into complexes containing several separate structures, which would all be known by the same house name. In fact, traditional names are often given to modern buildings on the sites of earlier ones. Houses could not, however, be erected in another part of the village since each family group owned a particular stretch of beach, but they could be

Below : On formal occasions a chief would sit in a settee decorated with his crests. This example comes from Bella Bella, a northern Kwakiutl village, and depicts an eagle, Thunderbird, whale and mosquito. It is basically an elaborate form of the backrests used as items of normal household furniture, but has added side panels.
Right, above : A totemic carving representing the salmon, the crest of the Kut clan at Kuthouse in the Tlingit village of Gunahho.
Right, centre : Great care was lavished on the decoration of even quite mundane items. Shown here is a Tlingit halibut fish hook carved with the image of a man holding a float over his head. The hook is made from cedar wrapped with cord and has an iron point.

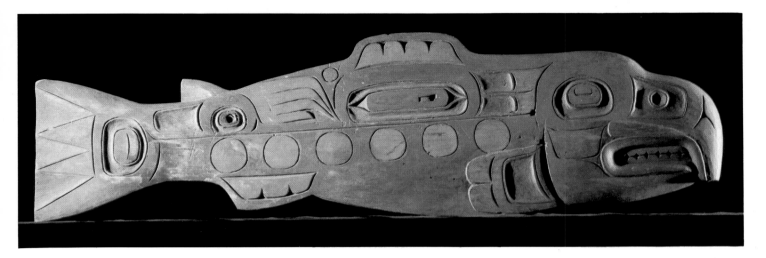

built behind existing buildings. In some of the old villages which had to cope with an expanding population this gave rise to two or three terraces of houses extending up the hillside.

Large villages were almost abandoned during the summer, when the people moved in small family groups to locations close to food sources where they erected simple brush shelters as temporary cover. Some of the main fishing localities had permanently standing log frameworks which were ready to receive planking brought from the winter site. The planks also came in useful during the trip, for by lashing them between two large canoes a fairly serviceable means of transporting freight was achieved.

Most of the summer was spent at these villages on the rivers and at the river mouths to take advantage of the millions of fish that were attracted to the coast by the Japan Current. Herring, halibut, cod, smelt, trout, perch and sturgeon, were all caught, and played such a major role in the economy that tribes as far inland as the prairies knew the coast dwellers as 'Fish-Eaters'. However, none of these was as important as the salmon. Perhaps the most typical feature of summer villages was the rows of salmon fillets laid on racks above the reach of the dogs and left to dry in the sun, or split open and stretched on twigs which hung above huge smouldering fires built all along the river banks. Even on the humid northwest coast, smoked and dried salmon will keep for long periods and a few weeks' work preparing the fish provided enough food to last for several months.

Before fishing began in earnest, the First Salmon Rite was held to thank the Salmon Spirits for providing food. The people believed that they swam up the rivers as a benefit to man and that this favour could be withdrawn, so it was essential to show respect and not to mistreat or kill them needlessly. Their bones were always returned to the river in which they had been caught in order that the fish would be reborn in the Salmon-Home-beneath-the-Sea. Great care was taken to ensure that no bone was missing since this would be absent in the reincarnated fish and cause deformity, thereby angering the spirits.

After this rite had been performed, weirs were built, sometimes spanning wide, rapid rivers, with catwalks along the top. They were made from a wickerwork of twigs and poles which directed the fish into various types of trap where they could be speared or netted. It was an extremely efficient method which provided vast surpluses to enable lavish feasting at the winter gatherings.

Sea mammals came close inshore following the shoals of fish, and were hunted not from necessity but as a means of proving skill, only incidentally adding variety to the diet. Seals, sea-lions and porpoises were plentiful, as were the smaller furry mammals like the sea otter which played such an important role in early trade.

Dead whales, which were then used by all the groups, were washed up on the beaches during the storms, and some whalers were believed to possess ritual powers which caused this to happen. These rituals were carefully guarded secrets involving shrines containing figures made from bundles of brush, and skulls and corpses which had been stolen from burials to represent the whaler's ancestors. A superstitious fear of the underworld made this link between dead men and dead whales particularly potent. In many ways the knowledge that a powerful source of help was near-by gave the northwest coast Indian the confidence to engage in decidedly dangerous pursuits, and this was no doubt true of harpoon whaling, which was regularly engaged in by the Nootka. They minimized the risks involved by enlisting supernatural aid through the performance of elaborate rituals in which the whaler mimicked the motions of his quarry and recited secret formulas.

Even with this help, however, whaling was not without danger. Since the harpoons were too unwieldy to throw with accuracy, the canoe had to be drawn alongside the whale to allow a thrust to be made, and the sudden roll and dive of the creature as the blade struck home required all the skill of the superb Nootkan seaman for him to avoid being swamped. Seal bladder bags attached to the harpoon lines acted as drags to weaken the whale, which was driven close inshore before being killed since it would have to be towed back to the village. As towing an enormous dead weight with a canoe can have been no easy task, the whaler's wife, back in the village, had the important role of enticing the 'fair lady' ashore through ritual prayer and will-power. She represented the creature and was believed to be able to influence its actions by her behaviour: if she lay quietly then the whale would cause no trouble, but any sudden movements on her part would make it restless and difficult to approach. A successful hunt provided more than enough food for an average size village, so it usually culminated in a feast to which neighbouring groups were invited.

The sea also provided plant life and a variety of molluscs, which were used for food and as a source of dentalia and abalone shell for inlay work, ornaments, and for use as household implements. In villages which had been occupied for several generations tons of discarded clam shells formed middens. These have proved invaluable to archaeologists who can locate abandoned village sites by their proximity. They provided a valuable food source close to the village as they accumulated a layer of rich, fertile soil in which berry patches and clover fields could be established. Crops were allowed to grow wild and collected when ripe, with individual ownership giving a person the right to the first, or perhaps the choicest, pick of the season, and limiting use to related family groups. Although some of the berries were eaten fresh, the majority were preserved in fish oil for use in winter.

Fish oil was, in fact, an extremely important part of the diet and no meal was complete without a bowl of it into which each mouthful of food was dipped. It was obtained from the eulachon, or candlefish— a small, sprat-like fish which is so oily that it can be burnt like a candle when dried. The Indians rendered the oil by boiling the fish in boxes or an old canoe (which was reserved for this purpose) and then skimming it from the surface of the water. Apart from its dietary importance, the oil was a valuable trade commodity which was exchanged between the groups. Most of them stored quantities of it for use during feasts as a method of honouring an important guest and as a demonstration of wealth.

As a very comfortable existence could be secured from the sea and supplemented by goods from the immediate neighbourhood of the village, there was little reason to venture into the dense, overgrown forests in search of game, even though this was abundant. Some bear, deer and elk were hunted close to the villages; the Chilkat, a Tlingit tribe, hunted mountain goats and used the wool for weaving blankets; mountain sheep horn was extensively used for bowls and ladles. It was,

Above : Fish oil was the universal condiment on the northwest coast and a bowl of 'grease', as it is commonly called, would accompany every meal Even today, dried and barbecued salmon is traditionally eaten with grease. It was also a valuable trade commodity and an indicator of wealth. This Bella Bella oil dish is carved in the form of a northern-style canoe.

Right : The Nootka obtained mountain goat wool through trade with the southern Kwakiutl and, since it was valued highly, only chiefs could afford to own blankets containing several wool weft strands. These were worn only on ceremonial occasions and displayed designs which represented the owner's privileges. This very early example of such a blanket was collected by Captain Cook in the late eighteenth century and is made from a mixture of goat wool and cedar bark. The design shows an oyster-catcher and a pair of skates. It is impossible to say that this blanket is definitely Nootkan, although it is probably so.

however, only the inland river tribes, with difficult access to the sea, who placed any importance on game as a food source. Bears' grease was in demand throughout the area as a cosmetic base to ensure the adherence of ochres and clays used in face and body painting, and was rubbed into the hair prior to sprinkling it with small white feathers.

Although as ship's hands they must have appeared a sorry, unshaven and grubby lot themselves, the sailors on board the European ships were too uncouth to recognize the inherent beauty of these practices and believed that the Indians were unclean. This was far from the truth. The Indians were accustomed to bathing daily and the grease and paint which so disgusted their visitors was used as an effective method of preventing wind- and sun-burn, as well as to enhance their beauty.

Artists travelling with the ships realized the value of the designs, and were greatly impressed by them. John Webber, who sailed with Cook, made paintings and engravings of the Nootka and noted that they were painting their faces differently each day and would sometimes turn up in the afternoon with a totally changed design from the one they had worn that morning. Other artists noticed that Haida face-painting repeated the designs used on their masks, and these have endured up to the present, giving some idea of the abstract symbolism involved in this form of decoration. In any form of body decoration the Indian's huge vanity was allowed full play, so that he might spend two hours or more applying paint and then decide that the standard was inadequate

The designs in Chilkat Tlingit weaving were copied by women from pattern boards painted by men. Since the boards were used many times over, near identical designs occur on different articles.
Left : Chilkat shirt with a design of the brown bear similar to that on the pattern board (far left). It is assumed that this shirt changed hands and was too small for its new owner : a gusset of otter fur has been added on each side to increase width.
Below : Tlingit weaving techniques were also applied to fine basketwork. Some of their baskets were so tightly woven that they could be used to store liquids.
Right : Portrait masks often had the same designs as were used in facial painting. This Haida mask would have been worn alternately with an animal mask to mark the character's transformation from a natural to a supernatural state.

and feel that it was necessary to repeat the entire process.

Other beautification treatments included the fairly widespread custom of tattooing, which had been discontinued by the early nineteenth century, and piercing the septum of the nose for the insertion of ornaments. Among the northern women, the lower lip was also pierced to accommodate a bone or wood lip plug, or labret, which might be as much as 7.5 cm (3 in) in width, to denote high status. The southern Kwakiutl and Nootka artificially flattened their foreheads by applying pressure from a padded board to the heads of their infants while in the cradle, and all of them perforated their ears from which numerous ornaments of copper and beads dangled.

A profuse number of different ornaments were worn all about the body, although bracelets were most common. They were made from any natural material that could be applied to a decorative purpose, such as copper, fur, bone, wood and iron. Generally the amount worn by any individual was decided by his or her social position. Other clothing was very scant. In fine weather the men frequently went completely naked, apart from ornaments, and women wore only a short woven apron. There was generally no footwear, even in the coldest weather. A great variety of rainwear developed because of the climate, and cedar bark cloaks and dresses were commonly worn during inclement periods. When these were covered with a bark rain cape, supplemented by a spruce root hat, the wearer was guaranteed to remain dry even in the most foul conditions.

Elaborate costume was only for ceremonial and socially significant occasions, when it consisted of masks and beautifully woven blankets of a mixture of bark and wool. This type of costume was undoubtedly worn by the man who greeted Cook with:

'A singular ceremony . . . conducted by a man dress 'd in a garment of many colours, to which is hung dears hoofs, pieces of bone etc in such a manner as to strike one against another at every motion of the body. This man is masked and shakes in [h]is hand a rattle, as do also some of the others, and if they had any masks with them they generally put them on.' (Cook's *Journal*, Notes.)

It is very probable that the person Cook referred to was an important personage in the village, since he dressed more elaborately than others on this occasion. But Cook did not find anyone who had absolute authority, or anything like it, although 'there are such men as cheifs who are distinguished by the name or title of Acweeks and to whom the others are in some measure subordinate, but I believe the authority of each extends no farther than over the family to which he belongs' (Cook's *Journal*, Notes).

A very sophisticated sense of belonging to a family group was part of every northwest coast Indian's character, and had evolved as the result of a long history of communal organization in which the community's needs were always considered before personal ones. Cook's Acweek would have been a leading member in a household containing several individual families, with as many as fifty members. It formed the most influential force in an Indian's life as it determined attitudes and established social position. The families were related according to their

method of reckoning kinship ties: northern groups were matrilineal; in the south they were mostly patrilineal societies, while the Kwakiutl in the central area, who form a transitional group, used both methods.

The households were formed of clan or blood relatives, depending on their locality. Both types were very similar, since clan members believed themselves to have a blood relationship. The household formed the basic social unit, which functioned independently in most matters among all the language groups. However, clans were more important in the north where there were activities which required the participation of several households.

Clan members believed themselves related through descent from a common legendary ancestor. The Tsimshian, who are typical of the northern tribes, lived in houses whose male members belonged to one clan group. Their wives belonged to different ones, because the northern law of incest forbade marriage within one's own group, and as descent was matrilineal the children followed that of their mothers. All the children of one woman, who had married three times, were members of her clan even though their fathers were Tsimshian, American and Chinese. Boys left home early and were brought up by their mother's family, usually by the maternal uncle, but a girl stayed with her parents until she married. Thus, the clans would be represented in several different households which were spread throughout the tribes.

Two or more clans might claim a further relationship between each other and form a tribal division. Each Tlingit tribe, for instance, had two divisions—Ravens and Wolves—within which were smaller clan groups whose members were more closely related: a Tlingit Raven would be a member of one of the twenty-seven clans constituting the Raven division. This relationship was traced back in the legends to a single household which had separated—according to the Tlingit, after arguments over women. In one of the legends from their Wolf division the wife of a chief was having an affair and feigned sickness, knowing that she would be secluded in a shelter during her illness and could have clandestine meetings with her lover. Somehow, her husband became suspicious and killed her paramour. The dead man's brother began a feud to avenge the death, thus scattering the chief's family over a wide area where, in accordance with tradition, they adopted new names and formed the numerous Killer-Whale clans in the different Tlingit tribes. Historically the separations were probably caused by population increase and expansion.

The Tlingit, Tsimshian and Haida formed a northern matriarchal sub-culture group and considered that their tribal divisions were related to each other. Thus the Tlingit Ravens were believed to be relatives of the Haida Eagles and of the Ravens and Eagles in the Tsimshian tribes; Tlingit Wolves were linked with the Tsimshian Wolves and Killer-Whales, and with the Raven division of the Haida. Theoretically, then, a Tsimshian Eagle might visit his relatives among the Haida Eagles, and even claim their support and protection, though they were complete strangers and spoke a different language.

In the central area only the northern Kwakiutl, with six linked clans, were similar to these matriarchies. In general, Kwakiutl clans were given less importance and were primarily local groups. Among the southern people the households were based on blood relationships, although this was sometimes interpreted very liberally. A Nootkan Ehetisat chief, for example, could consider all the sixteen Moachat groups as 'relatives' on the strength of a remote connection with one of them, but the Salish, by way of contrast, only maintained ties with other very closely related groups who had a direct connection through marriage.

Such closely knit groups, with a dependence on community co-operation, needed some form of sanction which could be used against members whose opinions were contrary to those of the group. Although

Above : Solid blocks of wood were carved into ceremonial crest hats. The killer-whale hat (top) is Tlingit and has abalone shell, human hair and sea-otter tooth decoration. Also from Alaska, and either Tlingit or Kaigani Haida, the eagle hat (bottom) is a superbly unified design.
Left, above : A human figure in foetal position with prominent or exposed ribs is common in northwest coast design. Birds and an otter surround the figure on this Cowichan spindle whorl and may represent spirit helpers of the weaver. Such whorls were used only by the Coast Salish groups and prevented the wool slipping from the spindle during spinning.
Left : The larger Tlingit houses had the floor space excavated to a depth of about a metre and doorways raised above ground level. Tiered planking provided space for sitting and was partitioned off for sleeping and storage. The carved housepost seen here is one of a pair supporting the massive ridge beams which are matched by a similar pair in the rear of the house.

the weight of group disapproval was normally sufficient to keep any anti-social behaviour within reasonable limits, if anyone became particularly troublesome they could be expelled. This form of control was one of the main reasons that the households could function efficiently while remaining independent, as it prevented factions developing within them. The social stigma of expulsion also stopped anyone changing group affiliation easily: another household would not readily invite trouble by accepting such a person.

Another aid to group solidarity was that every household and every clan possessed its own history and traditions in the form of myths and legends. These told of the connections and associations of an ancestor with the supernatural, often describing how he had met a supernatural being, in animal form, who had given him the ownership of certain privileges. These privileges were a highly important part of Indian life, and would be retained by particular family groups through their laws of inheritance. Privileges were what gave an individual status in the community. They were regarded as property, owned by the individual and by the group, and were valued much more highly than any material possession. In reality they were rights, such as the right to use a name, the right to perform a dance at a ceremonial, or the right to wear a special mask. Although the content and form of these were familiar to everyone through their being exercised in public, use was strictly limited to the current holder.

The Tlingit and Tsimshian Killer-Whale legends are very typical of these privilege tales. Natcitlaneh, in the Tlingit stories, was abandoned on an island by his brothers-in-law, who were jealous of his prowess in hunting. He was rescued by the Sea-Lions and taken to their home in a cave where, in gratitude for his healing their chief, they gave him supernatural power which enabled him to carve eight wooden Killer-Whales. These came to life when they were placed in the sea, and avenged him by killing his brothers-in-law. As a mark of respect Natcitlaneh built a house and named it Killer-Whale House. According to the Tsimshian tales, the ancestors visited the Killer-Whales' home beneath the sea and obtained the right to use the Killer-Whale as a crest. This right then became the property of several related households.

Since the supernatural world with which these histories dealt was not confined to physical limits, their credibility was unimportant, but, because they conferred privileges, they were always taken seriously. The supernatural animal beings in them are known as totems, and these were carved or painted in the manner of crests to represent the ancestral claims. They do not, however, claim descent from an animal, as is a fairly common theme in the legends of some other North American tribes.

Probably the most familiar form of these crests is the totem pole, which is unique to the northwest coast, and this term is applied generically to poles serving a number of functions. They were erected as memorials showing family lineages or to commemorate special events; they were used for mortuary purposes, the coffin of a deceased chief resting in a fork at the top or his ashes secreted in a cavity; they also served as house entrance poles with a hole carved through the base forming a doorway. A few entrance poles made by the Kwakiutl were elaborate constructions with hinged entrances. A person might enter the house through a large carving of Raven's beak which was then closed behind him by a complicated system of weights and pulleys.

All totem poles had a number of crests on them. One of the Tlingit totem poles, for example, had the owner's Sea-Lion crest carved as the topmost figure, with the figure of Raven (his tribal division) and Frog below this. The Frog was honoured in this way because of an incident in the clan history concerning a woman who had insulted one of these creatures and had been taken to the Frog-People's home as a punishment. When her own people rescued her, she was unable to eat human food and

soon died. The Frogs had demonstrated their powers, and were therefore used as a crest to prevent the same misfortune happening again.

It was usual for the top carving to represent the ancestry of the principal occupant of the house, while lower ones showed that of his wife's family and referred to details in the family history; several other carvings were the personal property of individuals and the crest of the tribal division was a further feature of northern poles. Since a lineage pole stood in front of its owner's house, a stranger could immediately recognize which families were connected with his own and where he might find food and shelter.

Crests were not, however, limited to totem poles, but were applied to everything. Carved, painted, or woven figures appeared on clothing, blankets, boxes, ladles, fish hooks, awls, weapons and ornaments. Anything, from the smallest utilitarian object to the complete side of a house, might carry a totem figure of some description: they would be superbly carved and painted on house posts and the Haida even had them tattooed on their bodies. All were used to demonstrate privileges, regardless of the type of object to which they were applied, and these were closely associated with social position.

The leading members of the households, whom we may conveniently call nobles, were those whose families had the right to inherit the most important privileges. Families without these rights, commoners, were lower on the social scale. Nevertheless, there were many degrees of rank within either class as positions were held individually, and the youngest siblings in noble families might even have commoner status as the positions of high rank were limited and inherited by the eldest heirs. At the same time, certain professions, such as wood-carving and canoe-building, were very highly esteemed and could only be inherited by commoners, which increased their social standing. Thus there could be almost as many degrees of rank within a household as there were individual members, giving the words noble and commoner (there is no direct equivalent for the Indian words) a tendency to mislead since the division is not at all precise.

Many of the groups had a special name for the highest-ranking member of the most important family. This word can be translated as chief. His power was nominal, since decisions were made by discussion with the heads of the various families constituting the household, but he had better connections with other leading families and was in a perfect position to act as his group's representative. Consequently, much of his time was spent in social engagements and he relied on his household's economic and moral support. He ensured getting it by giving frequent feasts and gifts, and his status was related to his generosity.

Also living in the houses were slaves, who, according to John Jewitt:

'form their most valuable species of property. These are of both sexes, being either captives taken by themselves in war, or purchased from the neighbouring tribes, and who reside in the same house . . . [they] are usually kindly treated, eat of the same food, and live as well as their masters.' (John Jewitt *Narrative* p. 99.)

Jewitt was writing about the Nootka, but the description applies generally to the entire northwest coast. Many slaves had been captured as young children and reared by the household, so they had knowledge of nothing other than slavery and spoke only the language of their captors. Although they lived in much the same way as anyone else, there was the major difference that they were never considered to be members of the family. As symbols of wealth, in the nature of property, they were very important, but not because they were productive. In fact economically they were as great a liability as an asset, since their productivity was unlikely to be much greater than their requirements. Their importance was the status they conferred on a chief, since he had

Left : A typical round, upright Haida Eagle mortuary post. A salal bush has established itself on this post, at the village of Skedans, and will eventually weaken the core, so causing the pole to topple.

Below : Marriage alliances are demonstrated on this Haida pole section from Ninstints village. The Raven crest of a bear with a cub between its ears is the main figure; emerging from the bear's mouth is an Eagle frog crest, while below this is probably a wolf—another Raven crest.

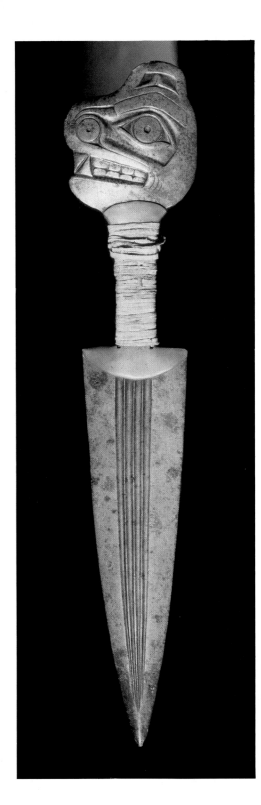

to be wealthy to support several slaves. Old Chief Shakes, of the Tlingit, is supposed to have kept more than seventy slaves, and it is even said that some of his slaves kept slaves. Jewitt notes that 'Maquinna had nearly fifty, male and female, in his house, a number constituting about one half of its inhabitants.' (*Narrative* p. 100.)

A further aspect of slavery was ransom, and people of high rank were often captured for this purpose. The reduction of a person's status to that of property was a disgrace which could only be removed by a payment of goods. Even should he or she be freed by force, goods still had to be distributed to wipe out the stigma. An excessive over-payment would remove this most thoroughly; furthermore, it implied that the captive's status was considerably higher than his captors had realized and raised the estimation of his, and his family's, worth in other people's eyes. If his own household was unable to raise the ransom, then his clan would be approached since the disgrace reflected on them also, though to a lesser degree. However, his captor might decide to assume his name instead of releasing him, as he could also do if no ransom was paid. This was a serious insult. Whenever the name was mentioned everyone would be reminded of the way it had passed into another group's possession, or that the captive's family had been unable to redeem him. The insult would be perpetuated for generations through the inheritance of the name.

A Tsimshian chief, wishing to insult another family, made a marriage proposal. His request was granted, but as soon as the ceremony was over he sold his wife as a slave to the Tlingit, and her family were forced to pay a ransom for her return. When he asked to marry her a second time her family dared not refuse, since they knew he had powerful relatives; thus she was sold into slavery and ransomed once again. He married and sold her a third time, but her family had used all their wealth and could not raise enough to secure her release. She therefore remained a slave, her family lost status, and a permanent disgrace became part of their family history.

Considerations of status played an important role in many aspects of northwest coast life, and were the major factor governing the arrangement of marriages. The stigma attached to marrying beneath one's own rank normally prevented commoners from marrying into the nobility, and such marriages were very unlikely to meet with public approval. Consequently, families attempted to match partners as equally as possible, and since households stood to gain or lose prestige according to the quality of the match, noble marriages were the concern of the entire kin group.

Some of the more powerful nobles attempted to increase their strength by forming marriage alliances with other powerful groups who were fairly distant, thus extending their influence over a wide area. This also suggested that there were no suitable marriage choices of sufficient rank in the immediate neighbourhood. Usually an important part of the ceremony was an exchange of valuable goods, the bride-price, which legalized the union and demonstrated the families' respective wealth.

These arrangements could become very delicate and complicated when the exchange was unequal, either in terms of goods or prestige. Among some Kwakiutl societies, for example, the women might inherit privileges which were exercised by men; thus, with patrilocal residence, the woman's family stood to lose more than they could hope to gain. To circumvent this, false marriages might be arranged with, for example, the foot of a relative in order to allow the privilege to be retained within the family group. Marriages between very closely related couples were made for the same reason.

Under normal circumstances, the marriage formalities were initiated by the groom's family (after lengthy discussions with the girl's kin) who held a feast at which they praised their son's qualities. Among the Haida, these speeches deprecated the groom's own family and

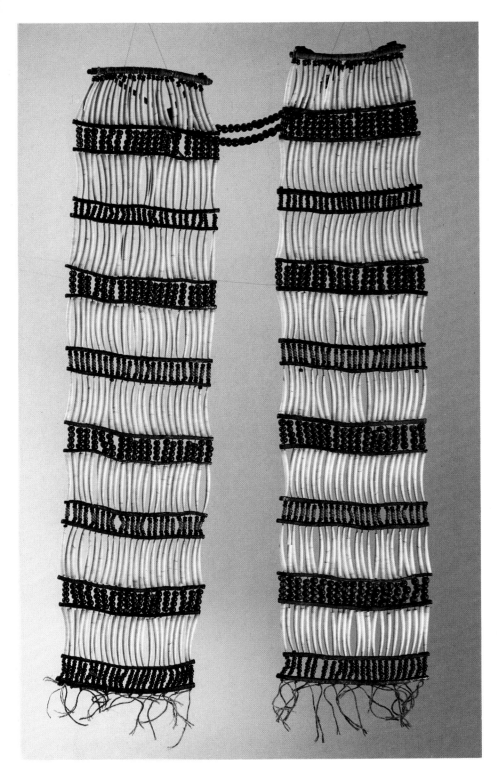

Far left: The hand-to-hand fighting characteristic of northwest coast warfare meant that most weapons took the form of clubs or knives. Although no iron or steel was used in aboriginal times, they were in great demand from the first white contacts. Hunting knives, bayonets and steel files were reworked into daggers by certain northern tribes, and iron blanks, used for the same purpose, quickly became an important trade item. This beautifully crafted copper and iron example shows the profile head of a bear and has been attributed to the Haida.

Left: Dentalia, or 'tusk' shells, were gathered in deep coastal waters by the Nootkans and valued as trade items. Here they are strung with glass trade beads as a hair ornament worn by pubescent Nootkan girls. The privilege of owning this type of ornament was restricted to certain chiefs; therefore, anyone wishing to use them had to make payment to the privilege-owner in the form of a gift. Depending on the user's status, they were worn for two to ten months, with their removal marked by a feast and potlatch after which the girl was considered marriageable.

extolled the girl's virtues, to which her relatives then replied with an apology for their daughter, saying she was unable to perform household chores and other wifely duties, but expressing their confidence that her future mother-in-law would be able to teach her. Following the speeches family histories were recited, with a display of the privileges they owned, and gifts were then distributed to the bride's relatives. This distribution was essential for families of any rank. Commoners could call on their household leader for support in obtaining the necessary goods, when they would hold a small ceremony. Higher-ranking families gave more lavish affairs and might have special marriage-canoes in which they would take the gifts to the bride's house.

The Nootka had a custom of refusing these marriage gifts three or four times. The refusal followed the speeches, which might have lasted a

Right : Among the Tlingit carved and painted cedar boards with designs showing ancestry and social position were fixed to the posts which supported the roof beams. The two fixing holes cut through the board can be seen quite clearly in this photograph. These interior boards were always made in sets of four which carried similar designs but depicted different aspects of the house group's history.

Far right : Kaigani Haida ceremonial robe worn by a chief at important occasions. Red cloth has been used to make the figure of a double-headed eagle and to trim this black Hudson's Bay Company blanket. The trim is emphasized by a double row of pearl buttons, while dentalia and abalone shell serve this same purpose on the central figure. Although shell was used for early blankets of this type, the majority are outlined with buttons— hence their popular name of 'button blankets'.

complete day, and meant that all the goods had to be carried back and forth between the beach and the girl's house several times. This practice was an indication of status, showing that the family was not too eager to marry off their daughter quickly because her beauty, virtue, and rank would attract many more suitors. The higher her social position the more refusals they felt obliged to make.

Only the Tlingit did not make a repayment of the bride-price, since the girl's family considered it to be compensation for the loss of a family member, but among all the other groups this was essential. Kwakiutl tribes might regard it as a competition and make increased returns, after which the wife was 'living in her husband's house for nothing', so he made another payment to restore her status. These exchanges continued throughout the couple's married life and were made at important events, such as the naming of a child.

As repayment of the bride-price for his daughter the Kwakiutl Chief Lagius contributed 600 blankets, 400 silver bracelets, sixty head-dresses, some boxes, brass bracelets, beads, bowls, and boxes with sea-otter teeth in them, towards the cost of a copper (a ceremonial plaque) worth the equivalent of 14,500 blankets. Lagius's share in the copper's purchase came to over 4000 blankets, representing a return of nearly 400 per cent on the bride-price. He transferred this to his son-in-law when his grandson, at the age of three, received a name given by Lagius.

A repayment which was considered inadequate would cause serious argument, since it raised doubts about recognition of status, which was directly related to the value of the bride-price. The son-in-law might give the goods to his own family, thereby suggesting that the amount was insufficient to be distributed among the local groups as was usual. Tardy payments were treated with contempt, as though the other family were too poor to afford them and unworthy of a continued association. A Kwakiutl husband carved a wooden image of his wife and, after tying a heavy rock around the neck, cast this into the sea from a cliff top as a sign of his disgust with her family for not having paid in time. She, of course, was not prepared to put up with such behaviour and left him.

Some of the nobles had several wives, which was a prestigious way of displaying their wealth since they would have paid large bride-prices for each of them. Ideally, a second wife was the younger sister of the first, as blood relations were supposed to get on well together, but most polygamous marriages were renowned for their disharmony, especially when the wives held different ranks. A highly ranked first wife might well resent her husband associating with a 'common woman', especially if she was younger and more attractive than herself. A number of second wives were inherited since the successor to a title took over responsibility for the deceased's wife and children. Marriage to female slaves was forbidden, though they were occasionally kept as concubines. Among the Tlingit, however, women held important tribal positions, and sometimes had several husbands.

In choice of marriage partner the nobles were obviously the most severely restricted class. Little attention was paid to their individual preferences when more important matters of tribal alliance and prestige had to be considered; use of concubines and the practice of polygamy suggest that the noble husband and wife were not always very close. Commoners had far greater freedom of choice, the wishes of sons and daughters being taken into account, and many marriages were affectionate ones. Indeed, frequent use was made of love charms and potions which were designed to make a girl fall in love with the young man who idolized her, or perhaps to make his seriousness obvious to her parents. Secret formulas for 'putting names' on a girl's ears, eyes, hands and head were used by the Salish to make it impossible for her to hear, see, touch, or think without being reminded of her suitor.

The restrictive concerns governing the nobles make it quite likely that divorce and infidelity among them was fairly frequent. Divorce was simple, merely requiring a change of residence, but could raise issues of insult and disgrace, particularly where one of the parties stood to lose prestige. Divorce was usual in cases where the wife was barren, because the birth of an heir was crucial, and in these situations a sister might replace her.

A husband could punish an unfaithful wife in any manner he thought appropriate, but she had the protection of her own household and he would have to be careful to avoid causing them any offence since they might retaliate if she were mistreated. They might also intervene on her behalf if her husband was guilty of infidelity but otherwise her only recourse was to leave him, in which case she would take personal marriage gifts and any young children with her. Although this type of dispute was often overlooked or settled by a payment to the aggrieved party, the most common reaction was one of outraged indignation which was soon forgotten.

There have been many societies which have used wealth as a means of gaining status, but there can be few which gave as much emphasis to this as those of the northwest coast. Their concept was not of hoarding or accumulating, except indirectly, since a person gained no benefit from it; their only concern was with the status obtained by showing a disregard for material considerations. The more material wealth a person was able to distribute, the greater his disregard for it could be seen to be, and, consequently, the higher his status. Theoretically, children inherited their status from only one parent, depending on the method of reckoning descent, and the privileges they received determined their social standing. So personal were these privileges that the Salish considered it an infringement of rights even to talk about those owned by another person. Privileges formed a special class of property which could not usually be given away, although in some instances one might be transferred to ensure that it remained within certain lineages. The right to its use had to be validated by gift-giving; therefore, material wealth was essential in determining a person's position within the community.

There were complicated arrangements for the ownership of various types of property, particularly in cases where a woman held it in trust for her eldest son who would inherit it when he was old enough. Certain types of goods had nominal owners, such as a household leader, but belonged to the entire community and would be transferred into the ownership of the new chief when he took office. Tribe, clan, household and individual all held powers of ownership. Those exercised by the group were divided into economic and religious categories, the household owning economic goods while the clan owned religious titles and paraphernalia. The household was often also the local clan group, and it was quite possible that actual ownership resided with exactly the same group of relatives. However, this might concern a particular section within the group, such as a certain dance order, or a number of men practising a definite profession like seal-hunting.

Individuals owned anything made and used personally, usually their weapons and clothing. Manufactured guns traded to the Indians initially belonged to the group but as they came into more common use ownership devolved to individuals. The letter was another type of individual property, and has a humorous aspect. Some white traders thought Indians dishonest, due to their practice of dyeing red fox fur black to increase its value and other similar tricks, and to counter this they presented them with letters of introduction which they were told to show to any other traders they had contact with. In the belief that these were complimentary, the Indians regarded them as personal privileges and displayed them with the other privileges they owned. The letters, of course, contained such compliments as: 'This Indian is the biggest liar and cheat in Alaska.' If he had known the true content, it is quite likely that the owner would still have used it for display, to show that

Left : Charles Edenshaw, the most famous Haida carver, made this cradle (below) for one of his daughters. His wife wove the spruce root cradle (above) and, since men painted the designs, it is likely that he was responsible for painting this crest. As the Haida were matrilineal, it is appropriate that Mrs Edenshaw's Dog-Fish crest is used on both these cradles.

Below : Functional design, the sculptured human figure holding a bow and arrow improves the balance of this Haida paint brush, which has bevelled bristles to permit the artist to paint both broad and narrow lines.

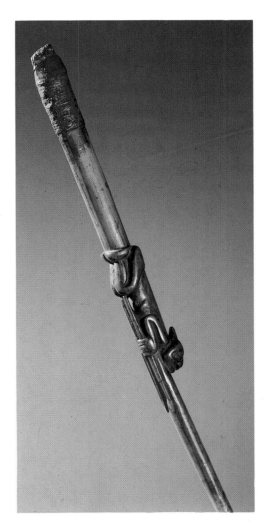

he had been singled out by the trader as important enough to write about.

The tribe itself did not strictly own anything, mainly because there were so many divisions within it, but insofar as the clan and household territories formed the tribal area, any unclaimed territory within that area could be considered tribal property. Important economic resources, the major fishing localities, for example, might come under the jurisdiction of several families who operated and exploited them on a communal basis, thereby giving the impression that they were the property of the tribe.

Personal names formed a more abstract type of property, but were nevertheless very strictly bound by the laws of ownership. At puberty an individual would take a new, adult name which belonged to the family and which would later be used by another family member, which explains why many successive chiefs were known by the same name. Ceremonial names were given at various stages throughout his life, and the more important people would be likely to use a considerable number of them. Many were actually titles referring to positions in the clans or societies, and winter names were frequently different from those used during the summer; any of them which had an associated privilege had to be validated through gift-giving.

The wealth goods necessary for validating these titles were given away during feasts—the actual giving being known as a potlatch—and these were often combined with a competition for status. They were most developed among the southern Kwakiutl, who would often hold feasts purely as challenges to a rival. In competitions between household leaders everyone became involved, since a chief who raised his status to that of Great-Chief also raised the household's standing above that of any other which lacked a similar claim to high title. Even within a single category of chieftainship there were ranked positions, and consequent household positions.

Since some of these feasts involved considerable amounts of property it was necessary to borrow. Generally the goods were provided by the local group, who stood to gain most in status, but they could be borrowed from the clan or from other related clans if the need arose. Loans were repaid with interest, which varied from group to group, and this was measured in terms of a standard of currency (since the latter part of the nineteenth century the Hudson's Bay Company blanket has been used as the standard).

A credit system in which small sticks served as indicators of the debt allowed these credits to be established, and the amount of goods on loan at any one time was far in excess of those actually in existence. The extent of the loans is obvious from this Kwakiutl example, among whom loans were repaid at one hundred per cent: in a village with a population of one hundred and fifty, there were four hundred actual blankets; the number on loan, however, totalled seventy-five thousand! Even so, a household could never become destitute by giving everything away, since the goods distributed were an excess of economic goods, and were used for no other purpose. At the distributions the hosts' privileges, or symbols of them, were displayed and the rights to ownership reasserted; titles were proclaimed; the histories of the families were recited; songs and dances were performed; and totems were paraded in front of the group.

In many ways this competition for status served as a substitute for aggression. Other than slave-raiding or feuds to wipe out insults, there was little fighting among the groups and, even in cases of feud, the affair was often settled by remuneration, the appropriate amount in goods being paid to compensate for the losses of the injured party. This substitution was especially true of the Kwakiutl, among whom many forms of feast and gift-giving, including marriage ceremonies, were known by words which refer to war. As one of their sayings puts it: 'We do not fight our wars with weapons, we fight with property.'

Below: The beaver in a sitting position on a section of a Haida house frontal pole. His prominent incisor teeth are very evident, as is the upturned cross-hatched tail which is here decorated with a humanoid face.

Right: Two Tsimshian monster crests, mythic creatures with human attributes, are seen on this pole section. At the top is Split-Corpse and below him is Nose-like-Coho (a type of salmon). This pole was the tallest in the village of Gitenmaks (Hazelton) and stood outside the potlatch house.

The Potlatch

The word 'potlatch' derives from the Chinook word '*patshatl*', meaning to give away. Potlatches were social affairs of great importance at which property was distributed as a demonstration of a man's ability to uphold a status position. The forms taken varied from tribe to tribe, but throughout the region they were essential in the establishment of what the northwest coast Indian held most dear, his social status. They were especially held where a claimant to a hereditary title and privilege was seeking approval of his claim, and were often given by a father or grandfather on behalf of a child. In these cases they passed on social responsibilities to younger generations, and with the privileges went a transfer of names, as announced in this extract from a potlatch speech: 'Look at me; look at my son! You shall not call me chief on account of what I am doing, but call my son chief, because I am doing it for his sake. I am working for him.' (Boas *Social Organization* p. 554.)

The importance of the privilege being transferred was measured in terms of piles of blankets. Before the introduction of trade goods these had been made of cedar bark and dog hair, or were animal skins and furs. The death of an animal was connected in the Indian mind with the spiritual powers which were held to be inherent in the name, symbolized by the giving away of skins in exchange for title. The animals had, in effect, been released from the physical world and could establish direct contact with that of the spiritual. By extension, this same principle came to be applied to any property given at a potlatch.

The most frequently held potlatches were small-scale affairs at which commoners or low-rank nobles marked important personal events. But there were also extremely lavish affairs, conducted around the rivalry of high-ranking families, which involved the participation of numbers of other tribes. Highly extravagant distributions honoured these great names—thirty thousand blankets were given at one nineteenth-century potlatch—and reflected the character of the claimant's ancestors as shown in their potlatch record. This was nowhere more obvious than in the potlatches held for initiation into a Secret Society, when important ceremonial prerogatives and names were transferred. These had aggressive qualities which made the potlatches highly competitive and antagonistic on some occasions, especially so among the Kwakiutl on the northern part of Vancouver Island, as can be seen from this speech and its reply:

'Friends, you all know my name. You knew my father and you know what he did with his property. He gave away or killed slaves; he gave away or burnt his canoes in the fire of the feast house; he gave away sea-otter skins to his rivals in his own tribe or to the chiefs of other tribes, or he cut them to pieces. You know that it is true what I say. This, my son, is the road your father laid out for you and on which you must walk. Your father was no common man; he was a true chief. Do as your father did. Either tear up these button blankets or give them to our rival tribe.'

'Did you hear what our aunt said? I will not block the road my father laid out for me. I will not break the law that my chief laid down for me. I will give these button blankets to my rivals. The war that we are having now is sweet and strong.' (Boas *Social Organization* p. 581.)

As their rivals were obliged to destroy or distribute an equal or greater amount in order to retain their status, such a challenge could not be refused without incurring a disgrace which their pride would not permit. People who received gifts at the distribution were thereby acknowledging their host's claims, so a major competition required a large audience as witness. Related tribes living within several days' travelling distance were invited months in advance. The potlatch began with their ceremonial arrival.

The visitors to the Kwakiutl potlatch waited in their ceremonial canoes behind the headland of the bay, out of sight of the village, until all the invited tribes had arrived. Then they approached the village together in a line abreast using a special method of paddling to keep their canoes' motions in time with the singing of their crews. The strokes of the paddles matched the syllables of their canoe song:

'Aw, ha ya ha ya hä
ha ya he ya ä
he ya ha ya ä
A, ha ya ha ya hä
aw, ha ya he ya hä
he ya ha ya hei
ya hä
hä hä wo wo wo.'

(Boas *Primitive Art* p. 314.)

One canoe from each clan, with a dancer standing in the prow representing his clan's totem, came in closer to the beach followed by the others; paddling became slower to keep time with the dips and turns of the dancers, and then stopped. The people in the line of stationary boats began beating rapidly on the gunwales with painted paddles which were held upright. Grizzly-Bear-at-the-Door-of-the-House-of-Cannibal-at-the-North-End-of-the-World Dancer, masked and completely covered

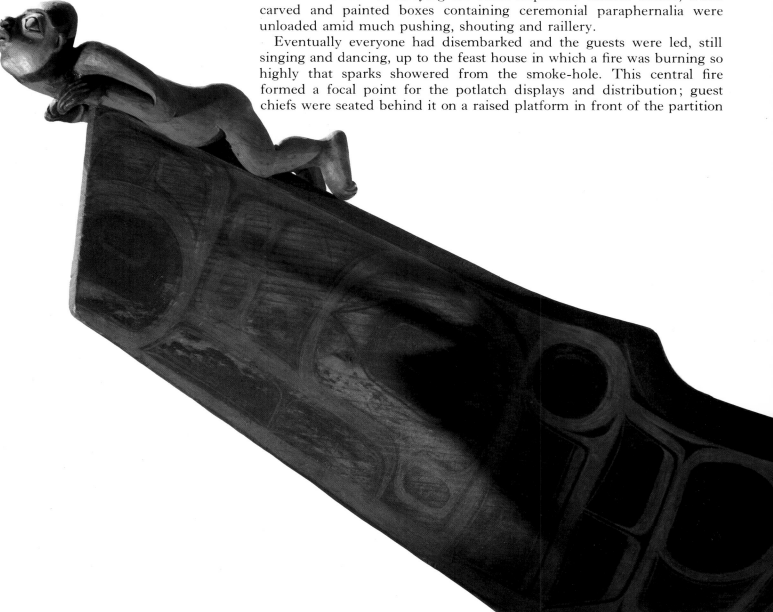

by a bear skin, started to dance energetically, using his arms to act out the movements of the bear, gesturing first to one side and then to the other. Although his feet remained motionless, his body moved so violently that it seemed almost as if he were jumping.

On another canoe, Eagle Dancer stretched his arms to the sides and then swept the wings of his feathered costume back horizontally. His movements were long and graceful, matching those of an eagle in flight, which made the rapid, jerky gestures of the Bear appear even more frenzied. Different figures danced with the other clans, so the affiliation of the people in the boats could be easily recognized.

Although the approach was made to honour the host, since it showed that his guests thought he was worthy of the performance, it was also self-glorification and ensured that the privileges embodied in the dances could not be overlooked. This attitude, in fact, underlay all the proceedings: status was achieved by asserting superiority over the guests, who were seen as rivals, and there was little prestige to be gained by competing with an obviously weaker rival.

Confusion and excitement reigned on the beach, where the people had crowded in to await the arriving guests. Some waded out to greet their relatives and old friends aboard the canoes which waited in the shallow water, their crews beating rhythmically with their paddles in time with the dancers. The host's family organized groups of young men for the task of carrying the more important visitors ashore, while carved and painted boxes containing ceremonial paraphernalia were unloaded amid much pushing, shouting and raillery.

Eventually everyone had disembarked and the guests were led, still singing and dancing, up to the feast house in which a fire was burning so highly that sparks showered from the smoke-hole. This central fire formed a focal point for the potlatch displays and distribution; guest chiefs were seated behind it on a raised platform in front of the partition screen, where they could obtain the best view of the proceedings. These seats were allocated according to social position; it was extremely insulting to show someone to a place beneath that appropriate to his rank, and a mistake might precipitate a feud. People were sometimes deliberately seated incorrectly in order to humiliate them by refusing to recognize their status, but an affront of this nature could not pass unchallenged.

The other guests found what space they could at the sides of the house, while the host's clan gathered about the entrance. Before any further activity commenced, the host made a formal welcome address during which he explained the purpose of the potlatch and spoke of the privileges which would be shown.

Speeches were important throughout the proceedings and were usually conducted in a manner which emphasized the speaker's superiority and belittled his rivals; it was almost as if the highest honour was gained by the person who delivered the greatest insult. They began by enumerating the various names by which the speaker was known; the more he was able to claim, the greater his importance was deemed to be since each had been validated by a previous potlatch. Typically, there would be an element of insult which would cast doubts on a rival's ancestry:

'That it is only the cause why I laugh, the cause why I always laugh at the one who looks around here and there, the one who points about for his ancestors who were chiefs.

The little ones who have no ancestors who were chiefs, the little ones who have no names coming from their grandfathers, who made mistakes coming from insignificant places in the world [and who are now attempting to go to high places through the potlatch competition].

Therefore it is only the cause why I laugh, the cause why I always laugh at the talk of these little ones, the chiefs who are [in rank] under our chief, tribes.' (Boas *Ethnology of the Kwakiutl* pp. 1282–4.)

The opponent had an opportunity to reply, and would attempt to undermine his antagonist's position by referring to him as an 'old dog' (a worthless creature) or a braggart:

'What will my rival say again—that "spider woman"; what will he pretend to do next? Will he not brag that he is going to give away canoes, that he is going to break coppers, that he is going to give a grease feast? Such will be the words of that "spider woman", and therefore your face is dry and mouldy. You will be like an old dog. This I throw into your face, you whom I always tried to vanquish; the chief whom even every weak man tries to vanquish.' (Boas *Social Organization* p. 356.)

Another recourse was sulking. Covering his face with a blanket he would turn round and stare at the wall, and his entire tribe would follow his lead. Their sullen attitude indicated disappointment at not having met an equal adversary, whereupon the host would taunt them until they considered the challenge worthy of their great name.

The competitive aspect of this potlatch lay in the host doing his utmost to cause his guests shame and discomfort while they attempted to thwart his plans. During the first three 'ceremonial days' (events took place in a set order over four 'days', but this was an arbitrary term and did not refer specifically to a twenty-four hour period; it might be longer or shorter according to the importance of the potlatch) status was claimed for an individual's lineage through re-enacting traditional events from his family history. As a result, although there were no written records, individuals were very well aware of their origin stories and ancestry; many Indians could trace marriage connections accurately over several generations—theoretically back to the creation of their world!

Not only did individuals trace their own histories carefully, but there was a check on their accuracy from the audiences witnessing the events and it is unlikely that unfounded claims to title would pass unchallenged. Origin stories were classed as property, each story belonging to a particular clan or family, and could, therefore, be demonstrated as part of the group's wealth by dancers who personated the mythological characters—such as Yaqalenala, a whale, who was one of the ancestor chiefs, or Grouse, the Canoe-Maker, who was the first person in the world to give away canoes at a potlatch.

Attention was concentrated on those parts of the histories concerning the acquisition of hereditary privilege names, which, of course, had

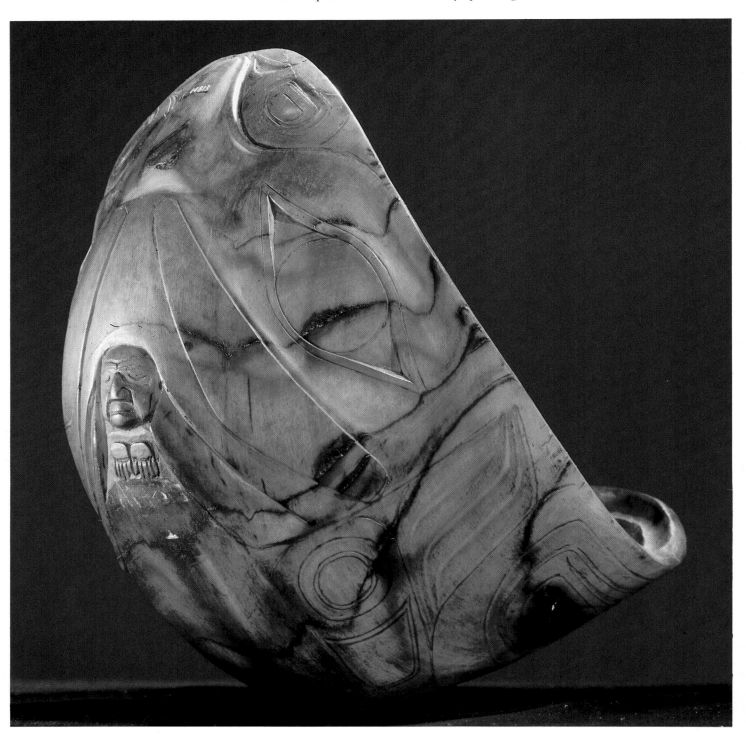

tremendous significance as they explained connections between powerful families. They were not entirely innocent historical references, but were used to emphasize clan and family superiority. Thus, a fairly typical speech, which had listed numerous marriages and liaisons with various tribes, concluded:

'Therefore I have many different names, because the chief, the root of my family, married in different tribes.

Therefore I am full of names and of privileges; and therefore I have many chiefs as ancestors all over the world; and therefore I feel like laughing at what is said by the lower chiefs, when they claim to belong to the chief, my ancestor.

The chiefs my ancestors married among the chiefs all around our world. This was not done by the ancestors of the lower chiefs, who approaches what was done by the chiefs my ancestors?' (Boas *Ethnology of the Kwakiutl* pp.839–57.)

His claim to status above that of his rivals, the 'lower chiefs', was quite obviously stated, although this had to survive opposition to have any meaning. The particular history from which this quote is taken traces twenty-three generations.

Interspersed among the recitations were eating contests. The host selected guests he wished to shame and set large bowls of food before them with the challenge, 'Now eat as well as you can, and eat it all.' The bowls he used were family heirlooms: the ceremonial house-dishes which bore names such as Tsonoqa, Beaver, Wolf, or Grizzly-Bear, and which had been carved from specially selected blocks of cedar. Each of these bore its own history of chiefs who had been defeated by failing to eat all it contained.

Sometimes bowls with tremendous dimensions, or even canoes full of food, were placed before a team from the opposing clan. Team members often climbed into the dishes to scoop up handfuls of fish-oil mixed with berries, and there were no rules to prevent fellow clan-members in the audience being pressed into involuntary service to uphold the clan's reputation!

Clearly it was essential that the host had more food available than would be required, and a large excess was a way of demonstrating wealth. This excess was extravagantly wasted in order to 'make his name great'. It was most exaggerated during that part of the potlatch known as the grease feast, when valuable eulachon oil was ladled on to the fire or trickled steadily into the flames from the mouth of a carving fixed to the roof beams and called the Vomitor.

The visiting chief had to sit beside the oil-fed fire and show no sign of discomfort, even though his blanket might begin to smoulder. Sometimes he pulled the blanket up to cover his face or lay face down on the

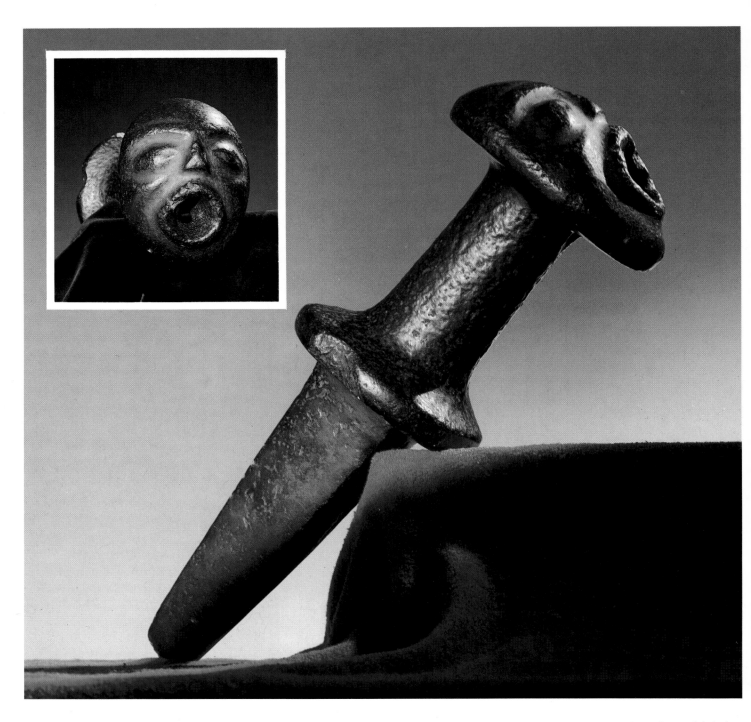

floor, thus showing resentment at being confronted with a fire which he did not consider to be a threat. He then sang an insult song to show how little importance he attached to his host's pathetic attempts:

'I thought another one was causing the smoky weather! I am the only one on earth—the only one in the world—who makes thick smoke rise from the beginning of the year to the end, for the invited tribes.' (Boas *Social Organization* p. 356.)

The song, of course, refers to the black smoke created by burning oil and to the grease feasts given at potlatches he had sponsored.

An incensed host ladled on more oil, and might send some slaves out to break a canoe into four pieces which he added to the blaze. His guest retaliated by sending for blankets with which he intended to smother the flames. The pile of oil-soaked property sometimes burnt so high that the roof beams were scorched or set alight, but neither chief took any notice since they did not wish to show weakness by being over-concerned about such material matters. Thus, the sponsoring chief, who had the right to have the flames extinguished, usually waited some time before taking any action and extensive damage would be caused, although Indian tales probably exaggerate in their references to houses burning down while their occupants ignored the flames.

On other occasions the guest might be ridiculed with a carved wooden figure, representing him in obvious distress and trying to shield himself from the heat, which was placed beside the normal fire kept burning throughout the potlatch. The guest, however, shamed his opponent and delivered the greater insult by enduring the ordeal of the grease-fed fire and then walking casually away when the flames had died down.

Most characteristic of the potlatch, and in actual fact the part to which the word specifically applies, was the 'give-away'. In a southern Kwakiutl potlatch this took place on the fourth day and was part of a longer series of recurring events in which obligations were met and new credits constantly being established. Goods given away at potlatches were always returned later when the original recipient held a potlatch of his own, but often he would give away more so as to place his rival in the position of a debtor. This, of course, put pressure on the recipient to return the goods at a future date and clear his reputation.

The chief urged his clan to make a concerted effort in accumulating enough property to substantiate his honour—and consequently that of the household—during speeches which compared their rivals to 'vast mountains of wealth' or threatened the imminent danger of 'being drowned by their property which ran from them in streams'. He made a contribution of his own and also called in outstanding debts from his relatives. These goods had been stored behind the partition screen or in different houses during the preliminary dances and contests, and they were now brought out and piled in the centre of the feast house while a tally-keeper called out their values. The object was to make as impressive a display as possible and sometimes, if the stories are to be believed, roof boards had to be removed in order to accommodate these piles.

Members of the host's family, wearing button blankets with crest designs outlined in mother-of-pearl, carried the gifts to the important guests, the highest in rank receiving larger amounts. All the guests received something, even if it was only a strip torn from a blanket as a token that they had witnessed the event. Consensus of opinion decided whether the potlatch had been successful, so everyone kept a careful note of what each person received and compared the values with those given away in the past.

Greater glory was achieved, however, by destroying property, since there would be no profit in the form of a return gift. Although this had tremendous advantages in that it cancelled all debts and placed the opponents in a decidedly inferior position, there was rarely wanton destruction of all the group's assets. Some blankets or furs might be cut up, and a canoe broken; sometimes a slave was killed with a special stone-bladed club known as a slave-killer, but he was more frequently given his freedom. Extremes were usually tempered by economic considerations and by the restraining action of clan members who did not wish to forgo their rights to return of their contributions. Even so, tremendous values were thrown away by the 'killing' of coppers.

These were shield-like plaques beaten out of raw placer copper (later replaced by European sheet copper) which was obtained through Tlingit and Tsimshian trade with Athabascan tribes in the northern interior. They had crest designs engraved through a coating of black lead, and as symbols of wealth were measured in terms of thousands of blankets, based on the prices paid when they last changed hands. Their names often reflected their values: Making-the-House-Empty-of-Blankets (used for its purchase), for example.

They were formally purchased at a potlatch, when respect was obtained by paying, say, 6000 blankets for a copper which formerly cost 5000—

Left: Heavy, stone 'slave killer' clubs, of which this is an example, may have been used on rare occasions for dispatching slaves during Kwakiutl ceremonies, although during historic times their use has been confined to cutting sections from copper plaques. Their shape is similar to that of the wooden wedges and steel-bladed tools used in copper ceremonies. The face with a perforated, circular mouth carries traces of red ochre, symbolic of blood, and suggests that this item had a ceremonial rather than practical use. Below: Whereas mountain sheep horn was used for large ladles and bowls, that of the mountain goat was employed for smaller individual spoons such as this one. Handle and bowl were made separately and riveted together. The delicate carving—a raven and doubled-up human here—made them valuable gifts to be handed to guests at the end of the potlatch feast in which they had been used.

Right, below: Copper plaques served as a unit of wealth and generally assumed the value of the number of blankets given away at the potlatch where they were exhibited. By being boastfully displayed at several potlatches, these 'coppers' could attain the value of several thousand blankets among the southern Kwakiutl. Most were named and decorated with crest figures. The beaver's incisor teeth and scaly tail identify the crest on this Haida copper.

Right, above: During the late nineteenth century, population decrease together with increased wealth caused an intensification of southern Kwakiutl rivalry for status positions. Possession of a valuable copper no longer guaranteed prestige; consequently, some coppers were cut into sections and the pieces scornfully handed to a rival, who had to accept them and the humiliation they implied. An irregular cut caused by a stone 'slave-killer' or copper-cutting tool with a wide blade can be clearly seen on the right-hand edge of this segment.

Above: As a wealth symbol, copper bands and strips were frequently attached to masks; but it was rarely that an entire mask would be made from this valued metal. This example was exhumed on the Queen Charlotte Islands in 1879 and is presumably of Haida manufacture.

the seller had to distribute the proceeds to his own tribe. At a future date this role was reversed and the tribesmen who had previously received gifts were called on to contribute towards the purchase price. This, of course, is over-simplified. Even after a price had been agreed the buyer might say, 'Do you think that is all I can afford? Here are another three hundred blankets to add to those I have already paid.' In this way he attempted to buy a symbol commensurate with his estimation of his own worth.

Each time a copper was sold its value increased, as did the prestige associated with using it at a potlatch. Thus, by validating a chief's name with a very valuable copper that name was 'made heavier' than if one of lesser value had been used. Even keeping one in the family brought honour to that family's house—it 'groaned with the weight of the copper's name'—and raised the estimation of their worth.

Coppers could be 'killed' in a number of ways: by being placed on the fire during grease feasts; struck in a ritual way; by being 'broken'; and by being thrown into the sea. The right to 'break' or 'kill' coppers was limited to certain very highly ranked chiefs and lineages—who boasted of their accomplishments quite freely:

'Nothing will satisfy you; but sometimes I treated you so roughly that you begged for mercy. You did so when I broke the great coppers "Cloud" and "Making Ashamed", my great property and the great coppers, "Chief" and "Killer Whale", and the one named "Point of Island" and "The Feared One" and "Beaver".' (Boas *Social Organization* p. 356.)

Breaking followed a strict ritual order and required five potlatches, since the copper was cut into five sections and these had to be formally presented, usually to five separate rivals (if they were all presented to the same rivals the copper would be 'killed'). This challenged the opponent's status and he had to match the act by breaking an equally valuable copper. He suffered tremendous shame and disgrace if he was unable to do so, and chiefs have even been known to die from worry as a result of not being equal to such a challenge. When the T-shaped ridge which formed the support was given away, at the fifth potlatch, the killing was completed.

The several pieces could, however, be collected and riveted back together. Because this required potlatching the various families who held the sections, a riveted copper had a greatly increased value, based on the number of ceremonies at which it had featured. They were only irretrievably destroyed by being 'drowned' in the sea, an action which had great associated honour.

Interestingly, their removal to ethnographic museums as a consequence of the Indian Act of the 1880s did not prevent coppers being used in status competition. The Indians, quite rightly, still considered them to be the personal property of rich lineages and used the names as symbols of the actual objects. Ownership of these names continued to be purchased and exchanged. Removal did prevent breakage and destruction, which had been so prevalent that few early placer coppers exist today.

Competition potlatching reached its most highly developed and exaggerated form among the Kwakiutl around northern Vancouver Island (from whom the preceding examples have been taken) and principally involved the leading members of opposed groups, with considerable moral and financial help. However, all the northern groups shared a similar attitude, and all had the same enormous concern for personal pride: it was just as important to the commoner who gave a few blankets to his friends when they witnessed his daughter's ear-piercing as it was to the chief who gave several thousand for a copper.

But if the Kwakiutl had one form of potlatching, and an extreme one, the forms it took in other groups were fundamentally the same. Tlingit rivalry compares with the Kwakiutl system except in a few areas of difference. The most important of these was that the entire local clan, instead of one clan-household, acted as hosts. This co-operation was taken to the extent that if a minor house wished to elevate its status it had the right to borrow a prestigious totem, in the form of a clan hat, from an important house in its own group, and this request could not be refused provided that the borrowers had sufficient wealth to uphold the totem's position. These conical basketry hats had crest symbols painted around them, and each time a chief wore one at a potlatch another cedar-bark ring was fixed to the crown, giving open expression to the clan's importance. Each hat had two names: its permanent name, such as Killer-Whale-Hat, and another which reflected the amount distributed when it was last displayed, such as Slaves-Halfway-around-the-Room and Two-Coppers-Facing-One-Another. The similarity between these and some names given to Kwakiutl coppers is not purely coincidence since the hats had the same prestige value, although they were not sold or exchanged. Tlingit coppers, on the other hand, had comparatively low, stable and standardized values.

During the Tlingit rivalry distributions only chiefs from opposite clans received gifts, and larger returns were mandatory only when the

potlatch had involved coppers or slaves. The slaves used in this connection were purchased immediately prior to the ceremony. They were usually Salish bought from the Kwakiutl, since the Salish lived at such a distance that it was unlikely for them to have relatives in the area who would raise objections. Household slaves did not feature in any way, not even as servers during the feasts; therefore, since the potlatch slaves were generally freed or adopted, this was really a method of giving away the equivalent of their purchase price. That the gifts were given to opposite groups is important, for these groups were also the labour force during memorial potlatches when new houses were built or totem poles erected, and were responsible for all funerary arrangements.

The Tlingit gave memorial potlatches, at which the titles and privileges of a dead man would pass on to a descendant. They were given in a series of four Mourning-Feasts and four Joy-Feasts which required six or more years to complete. The first Mourning-Feast included the lying-in-state and cremation of the deceased. Gifts of food and tobacco were given as payment for the attendants' services, which included removing house planks and carrying the body out, which, since his last exit could not be through the door used by the living, was through the side of the house. The attendants also had to collect wood, attend to the funeral pyre, and recover the bones from the ashes, which were to be preserved in a box at the grave-house. The other three feasts in the Mourning series were opportunities for glorifying the deceased's qualities and making claims to his titles. These were completed within a year and required giving away quantities of blankets; however, no returns of these would be expected, and they were sometimes torn into strips as tokens of witness. Completion of mourning was signified by the dancers who knelt silently on the floor for several minutes, and then thrust upwards at the smoke-hole with their dance batons to 'push away their sorrow'.

Joy-Feasts followed, sometimes several years later, which were associated with raising a memorial. This could be a simple grave-marker or a major task such as house-building. Throughout these, members of an opposite clan division laboured and received food and potlatch gifts in payment; their chiefs, who did no physical work but acted as overseers, were paid for their ceremonial services. Although none of the property given away during this series was returnable, it would be recovered when the sponsoring group was asked to perform similar

Stone carvings were produced by the laborious process of pecking at the surface until the desired form was achieved.
Above: Haida tobacco mortar.
Right: Tsimshian stone mask.

62

duties. Thus, the potlatch was an economic exchange which strengthened tribal solidarity and forced interdependence on groups who were at other times in direct competition with each other.

The Tsimshian had a very similar series of connected ceremonies, frequently associated with the replacement of old totem poles which, because of the damp climate and soil, became rotten at the base after about fifty years. As in all potlatching, the recitation of history was important and lengthy speeches retold the stories and explained the symbolic meanings of all old poles belonging to the clan, thereby conveniently instructing each new generation. It is easy to mistake the many fallen and rotting poles at old Indian villages as proof of neglect, but this would be entirely erroneous. There was no prestige attached to repairing a pole which could cost as much, in terms of potlatch gifts, as the prestigious affair of raising a new one. Therefore, old poles were left to decay and their symbols were recarved.

Neither the Tlingit nor the Tsimshian carried their potlatching to extremes. Although several small potlatches might be held in one year, nearly all were intra-village or among local villages and only rarely were the large inter-tribal affairs held which were so essential to the Kwakiutl. In fact, the only ones which were considered to be major were those given to commemorate the deaths of important chiefs.

The Haida chief borrowed the goods for his potlatches from his wife's family, who would be members of the opposite clan division, and gave back to the chiefs who were clan leaders in his own group—a complete reversal of that practised by most other tribes. It was only on the occasions at which a grave-marker was being erected that visiting guests received the main distribution since it was their duty to supply the labour, as among the Tlingit. A record of potlatching was kept on very obvious view in the form of carved rings which encircled the Haida memorial poles and made the owner's status evident to everyone.

The competitive element was missing amongst the Nootka and Salish, for whom social recognition was achieved through the mutual acceptance of rights. Nevertheless, the potlatch was still essential at every change in social relationships, which had to be formally presented before an invited group from outside the family circle, but it was a very great disgrace if any ill-humour developed and these were occasions for festivities and friendly contacts. The Nootkans expressed this by saying, 'You couldn't fight or quarrel in a potlatch. That would give a bad name to your child, and be a disgrace to your whole family.'

Nootkan feelings can be contrasted with the Kwakiutl's in this example of a guest who had been seated incorrectly. He remained in the wrong seat to avoid causing his host the embarrassment of having to ask other guests to change places; nevertheless, he wanted to be certain that his correct status was known by all so he announced that a mistake had been made. As an apology for having made the blunder public, he then gave his host and one or two other people gifts. Later on he would be singled out as the recipient of a special gift which would atone for any indignity that he may have suffered. This same procedure was followed whenever anyone suffered discomfort through his host's negligence, such as by stumbling on an uneven floor, or having water drip on him.

Although they had no competition, the Nootkans were very rank-conscious. Their chiefs formed a definite élite and were addressed with special terms of respect to differentiate them from other members of the households. They even dressed with greater splendour than their fellow tribesmen on important occasions. Though they were a 'royal' class, their authority extended no farther than over the local group.

In marked contrast, however was the humility of Salish chiefs. They earned respect by quietly expressing an opinion after everyone else had their say, by not boasting or dressing flamboyantly, and above all by being generous. In fact, their chiefs were often recognizable because they were the most poorly dressed members of the community, as they

Below : Many Haida poles had three 'watchmen' figures carved at the top who were said to cry out a warning if danger approached. These figures wore ringed 'skil' hats. Sometimes only one figure was shown wearing a 'taden skil' (long hat) indicating that he was an important chief ; on other poles he is flanked by one or two smaller men with skil *hats showing that he would be succeeded by one or two brothers.*
Right : A recently fallen Haida mortuary pole at Skedans, carved with a bear crest, which once stood as a memorial to an important member of the Raven division.

had given everything away to retain the support of their followers. During their potlatches social position was tacitly assumed and insulting speeches were absent, but this was accompanied by the expectation that return gifts would be larger.

A rather curious custom followed the formal gift-giving in the southern part of Salish territory; this was the scramble. Goods, or tokens of them, were thrown from a platform erected against the wall of the Long-House or were dropped into the house through the smoke-hole. Everyone, of any age, rank or sex, vied for possession. Quite often a scramble formed part of the marriage ceremony, when the bride's 'seat'—the pile of blankets on which she sat during the formalities—was thrown out. Although the free-for-all was friendly, it was likely that the blankets would be cut up and destroyed if the people thought that the chief was not being generous enough, but generosity was so vital to a Salish chief's prestige that this can have happened only rarely.

Although often connected with religious ceremonial, the giving-away of gifts had no religious meaning. It had a ritual function during these ceremonies, as a dancer could not be initiated without first validating his right to a position by potlatching, but the performance of religious dances during property display was essentially a demonstration of ownership and not of religion. It may, however, have been symbolic: excessive destruction of wealth has a parallel in the voracious Cannibal Spirit, who consumes vast quantities of human flesh. He is the most important dancer in Kwakiutl ceremonies, and also appears in the dances of many other tribes. Furthermore, smothering the rival's fire compares with overpowering the spirit forces, and vomiting, caused by nausea from the vast quantities of eulachon oil they consumed at potlatches, is frequently considered analogous to birth—the use of oil as

part of the bridal gift to 'make her name heavy', or valuable, reinforces this: prerogatives passed to children and barren wives were worthless.

By the mid-nineteenth century the potlatch blankets of native manufacture, made of cedar bark, and of dog and goat hair, had been almost completely replaced by woollen Hudson's Bay blankets obtained in trade. In addition, other goods, such as furs, canoes and carved boxes, were given blanket-values: a canoe was worth, say, 700 blankets, or a sea-otter robe thirty. Some trade goods had probably been introduced with the earliest European contact, and by the end of the century such items as wash-basins, copper kettles, and sewing machines formed a major part of the distribution.

Blankets were used as the unit of currency, making the measurement of return goods easy. Increased wealth, through white trade, made the acquisition of them in great numbers possible for both the nobles and the rich commoners, since trade goods were available to anyone and were not dependent on allegiance to a particular household group or leader. Also, the decimation of native population through disease meant that the strictly limited number of prestige positions began to exceed that of noble claimants, and commoners started to lay claim to these on the basis of remote family connections. Moreover, they had the wealth necessary for validating these claims. Other seats were held 'in trust' by women with no male relatives to pass them on to.

The effect of this was to increase competition until the centuries old system of social organization began to break down. On the other hand, it simultaneously channelled aggression away from war. Early traders reported almost universally peaceful relations with the tribes

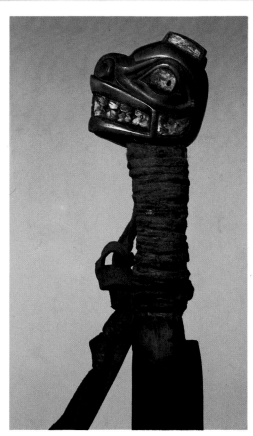

they met, but it is possible that war had previously made potlatch goods available in the form of booty and that trading made this unnecessary. Younger siblings of noble families, whose elder brothers inherited the status, had been able to gain respect equal to that of their brothers by killing the owner of a privilege and assuming his position, which suggests that they already knew all the ritual associated with the privilege but had to establish a right to its use. Where these privileges had been obtained in the past by killing their owners, this could now be accomplished by potlatching for various positions.

War, in the northwest coast sense, was any conflict between two or more individuals and did not always involve physical violence. It ranged from a metaphorical slap in the face to a pitched battle involving hundreds of armed warriors. Mostly it was feuding, related to removing a slight or insult by proving who was the stronger of two antagonists, and 'battles' might be decided on the basis of oratory, with those threatening the most horrendous consequences emerging as the victors. Kwakiutl speeches actually seem more aggressive than their methods of warfare, and it is possible that much of it was bluff, show and challenge. Possibly it was used as a way of raising the group's status by presenting a terrifying aspect to the outside world in order to gain the respect of neighbouring tribes. Indian wood slat armour was surmounted by a wooden mask which made the warrior appear about two metres (seven feet) tall, and this mask was carved with a human face depicting a frightening visage—confirmation of the 'terrifying aspect' tribes sought to attain.

Initially, trade contacts with Europeans brought a short-lived increase in inter-tribal warring, which became quite lethal with the use of muskets, and resulted in the Kwakiutl even holding a war season during which they slept on the roofs of their houses to avoid being massacred in a surprise night attack. But war was a thing of the past by 1860 and white cultures were rapidly undermining traditional culture.

European concepts of property ownership and investment were diametrically opposed to the principles which underlay the potlatch, and white colonists were unable to tolerate this questioning of their attitudes. The potlatch ban incorporated in the Indian Act was fully in effect by the early 1900s when government agents were operating on the reserves and attempting to break up any distributions of goods. The last major potlatch, that of Daniel Cranmer, a Kwakiutl from Alert Bay, was held in 1921 at Village Island, which was chosen as it was a remote spot away from government interference. But the identities of the people who attended were discovered and they were ordered to surrender their potlatch paraphernalia. Boat-loads of ceremonial goods were confiscated from them and others and cheques were presented to the owners in 'payment' for this, although some of these were defiantly torn up in the faces of the government officials.

Potlatches continued to be held secretly but they were only a shadow of the former affairs. Many people were afraid to attend them through fear of imprisonment and the verbal histories of the tribes began to break down and lose their continuity. Attempts at a revival in 1944 were a failure since people were still afraid to express open defiance of the agents. When the potlatch ban was repealed in 1951 serious damage had been caused to tribal identities and social stratification.

Today, agreement has been reached in principle for the return of the confiscated property, so that at least part of a national heritage will be returning to its homeland where it will be under the control of a tribal council. But, this is only a fraction of the original goods, as the agents kept much of it for themselves and more has been scattered in museums throughout the world. Perhaps some day soon the spirits of Tsonoqa, Cannibal-at-the-North-End-of-the-World, Hoxhok, Sisiutl, Toxwid, Raven, Crooked-Beak-of-Heaven, Hamatsa, and many many others will be free to roam again in the world they lived in at the beginning of time.

Left, top : Crooked-Beak-of-Heaven, identified by the curve over the upper beak, was a fearsome monster bird which the Kwakiutl believed lived in a house in the sky. It was known to fly to earth where it consumed men, and its mask was worn by women during the Hamatsa dances.

Left and above : The standard coast warfare tactic was a surprise attack at night when the warriors crept into an enemy's house and waited beside their chosen victims, knives and clubs poised, for a signal to strike. The aggressively carved bear's head on a classic Tlingit fighting knife (left) matches the use to which this implement was put. A fine example of an early Nootkan club (above) is elaborately carved and decorated, but ideally suited to this type of encounter. The leather thong secured the weapon to the user's wrist, and the carved ridges at the base of the shaft ensured a firm grip.

The Supernatural

The Indian shared his world with a profusion of spirits whose presence was reflected in every aspect of his life. These spirits manifested themselves in various ways and were seen as fulfilling different functions: some came with privilege rights as totems, some concerned themselves with everyday life, and others conferred powers on the shamans and sorcerers.

Everything possessed power, or spiritual force, be it a pebble on the beach, a rock, tree, animal, or man himself; abstract qualities, such as beauty, had a similar force, as did the sun, moon and stars, and the lakes and rivers. Although this power originated in the spirit-world, it manifested in the realm man occupied. The wind whistling through the trees, the creak of tree trunks, and the roar of underground waters, were all suggestive of the close proximity of some spirit. Bird and animal behaviour, and the changing patterns of the sky, were considered as signs given by those influencing the weather. Certain rock formations, lightning-struck trees and so on, indicated the scenes of supernatural occurrences. These all provided tangible evidence of the spiritual world, and directly connected it to man.

His affinity with his environment helped give strength to the Indian's beliefs. These were not remote, vaguely formulated superstitions, but

Left : Symbols of mystery. Petroglyphs and pictographs may denote the places at which supernatural encounters were believed to have occurred.

Above: The devilfish, or octopus, with its long, sucker-covered tentacles is seen in this detail from a painted caribou-skin shaman's robe. Undoubtedly the devilfish was one of this shaman's spirit helpers, and his other contacts in the supernatural world were also those of the 'tekijek' or water spirits: a killer-whale features as the central figure in the robe's design, and the devilfish is balanced by a painting of a whale on the opposite edge. The robe was collected from the grave-house of a Tlingit shaman from the Hootz-ah-tar tribe.

Right: A Haida mortuary pole from Skedans. Burial rituals were carefully observed among all the people of the coast, and memorials such as this were erected to show respect to the spirits of the dead. Even so, these spirits could become malevolent, and then their presence in the dense forests was a constant threat to the unwary. Among the Haida they assumed the form of a Ga-git: a monstrous creature with a hair-covered body, claw-like fingernails, and the ability to fly.

were real, potent and constantly present. Even though he was bound to the natural world by his physical presence, he was not prevented from communicating with that of the spiritual during dreams and trances. Moreover, since the supernatural was essentially an extension of the real world, with its presence indicated by a number of natural phenomena, he believed that a physical meeting with a spirit was quite possible.

Many of these were personified. They were the supernatural beings which lived in inaccessible places deep in the forests, under the seas or on the mountains. The forest land, with which these people were least familiar, was inhabited by vast numbers of dangerous beings with a propensity for causing harm. Typical of these was Tsonoqa, the Wild-Woman-of-the-Woods. She would eat any children she was able to catch, constituting a serious threat to any children who might wander far from the village and become lost. Although she slept most of the time, when she was awake her presence was announced by a whistling noise in the trees. In the mountains was Baxbakualanuxsiwae, the Cannibal-at-the-North-End-of-the-World, whose household included a woman who enticed men indoors and then killed them, a man-eating bird with an immense beak, and a Supernatural-Grizzly-Bear. Quartz crystals hummed and vibrated in forest caves and had the power of killing men; and shamans often kept small pieces of quartz for their supernatural properties and as evidence of their contact with the spirits.

Although they too possessed powers for evil, the beings of the rivers and inlets were in general less fearsome since their evil attributes could be suppressed through rituals. There were numerous water monsters which were believed to be responsible for endangering the seas; giant squids and supernatural sharks lived in deep rock pools, where Nootkan war chiefs bathed to demonstrate their invincibility. Even so, a meeting with a water monster was not particularly feared as such was the Indian's familiarity with the sea that it was thought that this was more likely to result in good luck than misfortune. A Kwakiutl meeting the double-headed sea serpent would receive the ability to perform magical tricks, and a Tlingit who met the sea monster Gonakadet was certain to become wealthy and occupy an important social position.

The monsters gave a form of reality to unknown or unpredictable forces, thereby making them easier to understand and cope with. Animals and animal behaviour, however, were very clearly understood and animal spirits performed more benign functions. The abundance of animal life was considered a gift from the spirits, and those on which the Indians were economically dependent were believed to sacrifice themselves willingly to man. They could do so since they would be reincarnated if the correct rituals were carried out, which usually involved returning their bones to the place where they were caught. Because the sacrifice was made voluntarily, it was essential to acknowledge their generosity.

First Salmon Rites were the most important of these rituals, but numerous others were held for the benefit of different animals: lengthy prayers and thanks were made to the carcases of whales which washed ashore, and to seals on the occasion of a seal hunt. When a bear's body was brought into the house it might be met and formally greeted with a welcome speech before being strewn with sacred eagle down. Sometimes it was even placed in a seat of honour at the rear of the house for a day or two and treated with all the respect shown an important guest, so that it would not be offended and its spirit would have no fear of returning to the vicinity of the village after reincarnation.

Special acts were carried out by hunters to please their quarry. The Salish goat hunter ceremonially painted his face with symbols he had received from the goat's spirit during dreams to ensure that his prey would not flee at his approach. It was the ritual act of painting rather than the painting itself that was effective, and it was a secret and personal

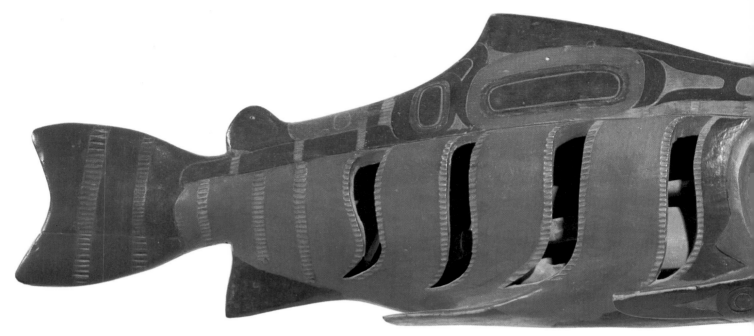

form of magic. If meeting another person was unavoidable the hunter would wipe his face clean, without this destroying the charm. He would make no attempt at a kill without this preparation as doing so would invite bad luck and destroy the trust he had established with the spirit.

These rites encouraged the animals to return to their homes with the news that they had been well-treated. The prayer of the salmon fisher helped to ensure a good season:

'Welcome, Swimmer. I thank you, because I am still alive at this season when you come back to our good place; for the reason why you come is that we may play together with my fishing tackle, Swimmer. Now, go home and tell your friends that you had good luck on account of your coming here and that they shall come with their wealth bringer, that I may get some of your wealth, Swimmer, friend, Supernatural One.' (Boas *Ethnology* p. 1319.)

That of the halibut fisher was recited as he struck the fish over the head with his club:

'Indeed, this does not sound bad on your head, Old-Woman, you Flabby-Skin-in-Mouth, you Born-to-be-Given-in-House, for, indeed, I came to do so to you with my club, Old-Woman. Go now and tell your father, your mother, your uncle, your aunt, your elder brothers, and your younger brothers, that you had good luck, because you came into this, my fishing canoe.' (Boas *Ethnology* p. 1322.)

The prayers were not directed to the actual fish, but to their souls or spirits, and the names by which they were called were all ones of respect.

If these formalities were disregarded, or the animals abused or insulted, then they might withdraw the privileges and fortune they gave— perhaps even retaliating more dramatically. In one village the adolescents had been tormenting fish by putting burning pitch into slits cut on their backs. The old men warned that this insult would bring retribution, but no one took any notice of them. Even when a distant rumbling noise was heard the young men only joked that the spirits must have empty stomachs. As the noise became louder the young people began to be more careful about their actions and comments, but they had heeded advice too late. The earth opened up and the entire village was destroyed.

Above, top : The close relationship between man and animal is made unusually explicit in this Tlingit salmon rattle containing an effigy figure of a shaman.
Above : Detail from a Tsimshian storage chest which was filled with a shaman's supernatural paraphernalia. Only after the coming of christianity would a shaman dare reveal his potent treasures.
Right : The Thunderbird appears during the sacred Tsetseka winter season of the Kwakiutl. Its mask is recognized by the feathered horns.

Of all the animals, wolves had the strongest supernatural powers. They were the most proficient hunters of the land animals and were respected for this ability. Since they might confer it on people, they were often sought as spirit aids by hunters—of whom the Salish believed they were the reincarnated souls. The Kwakiutl considered them as ancestors and frequently personated them in religious ceremonial. Their spirits were, however, harmless to man, in contrast to the innocuous owl and land-otter, both of which were greatly feared because of their association with the spirits of dead people.

Certain animals were used as totems and had a closer relationship with the people in the clan which used them as a crest. There was no tabu restriction on killing an animal from one's own totem group; in fact, it was often considered easier to do so. A woman from a clan using the Land Otter crest, for example, might have powers to talk to her 'relatives' who could be persuaded to ensure adequate food supplies, and a hunter in the Bear clan had less fear of attack on a bear hunt.

The totem spirits appeared only once, in the mythological tales telling of their contact with a group's ancestor, and thereafter remained present but unmanifest. Their power was symbolically expressed in the forceful paintings and carvings of the totems. They were an important feature

of the rank system as the display of totems proclaimed the status of the individual or group which owned it, which was thereby showing the spirits with which it was linked. But they also had a mystical quality which connected the symbol with the power of the supernatural being which it symbolized: a carved and painted box with a Bear symbol was seen to be imbued with a Bear spirit which protected the box's contents.

The totem spirits, whose origins were recorded in myth, were quite distinct from the supernatural spirits whose presence was constantly apparent to man. Finding pieces of mica which were believed to be the scales of Sisiutl, the double-headed serpent, gave proof of its existence, which was reinforced by the dangers it supposedly caused at sea. The Thunderbird, described as a giant bird which caused thunder when it moved and which kept reptile-like lightnings 'as a man keeps a dog', was believed to be the supernatural cause of thunderstorms and was regularly seen in the heavy rain and storms of the coast.

Man had good reason to fear the mysterious powers of these ever-present forces, but he could also use them to his advantage, as in the acquisition of hunting ability or fishing skills. They might bring him good luck, and allow him to foretell the future or predict the outcome of war; some gave him control or influence over the weather; a few granted shamanistic healing powers, while the majority simply afforded a degree of personal protection against the evil inclinations of others. But they were not naturally benevolent and did not confer these powers indiscriminately.

Power had to be sought and the spirit controlling it had to be challenged and dominated to persuade it to bestow its power upon man. This involved direct contact with the spiritual force, in either a trance or a dream. It was a potentially dangerous undertaking since an inadequately prepared person was liable to become possessed, and the Indian's belief in the effects of spirit possession made insanity or death, sometimes after prolonged and delirious illness, almost inevitable in these cases.

Ritual bathing was employed as a means of obtaining protection since it cleansed the body of human odours which were considered offensive to the spirits. Bathing lasted for a period of several hours in ice-cold water on each of a specified number of days, generally four, and was undertaken during particular phases of the moon. Following bathing, the body would be rubbed vigorously with branches or plant stems—often so violently that blood flowed freely—using those from the sweetly scented species so that any human traces would be disguised by their fragrance. From a practical viewpoint, this rubbing restored the blood circulation.

The bathing place, length of the ritual, phase of moon, and types of plant used, were all family secrets, which were carefully guarded against use by others since their efficaciousness was derived from the performance of a precise ritual order, which could be imitated. In contrast with their usually co-operative nature, the Indians guarded this information jealously because the exercise of these powers, being family property, had a certain degree of prestige associated.

Many people followed regular bathing rituals for their beneficial effect on health and luck, and as a safeguard against an accidental meeting with a spirit, but they were often used as part of a deliberate search for power when they would be combined with an almost total fast. The seeker, in a semi-conscious state from lack of food and loss of

Tsimshian carved wooden seal mask with copper eyes and operculum teeth said to have been used in a dance which preceded the execution of condemned prisoners.

blood, and perhaps also suffering from the effects of exposure, was resolved to meet a spirit, and was quite likely to be successful. He bathed in spots where they were supposed to dwell, offered long formulaic prayers to them, and encouraged them to appear with gifts of sacred eagle down.

Although not every spirit-quest was successful—some people searched all their lives without receiving any supernatural gift—if it was, the first sign was an unusual noise which would attract the person's attention. Turning to look, he would catch a glimpse of a supernatural animal, perhaps a squirrel or a mink with something strange about it which suggested that it was not a natural being. Then he would feel suddenly light-headed and usually faint. A person who was well-prepared would have time to give a shout and perform a ritual act, such as striking the creature with a stick, before fainting away. This act was known as 'killing' the spirit and persuaded it to leave a token containing its power. If it was well disposed it might leave the token without being killed, and this ritual could then be performed upon recovery from fainting.

The spirit returned later during dreams to explain the type of power it had left, and to teach the songs, dances, face-painting, ornaments, and so on associated with it. The token was all-important, for what the person received was really the ability to dominate a supernatural force, which he was able to do through its use. If he lost his token then he also lost his power. He would practise using it for anything from a few months to several years, depending on the strength it had, before he felt confident of controlling it and being able to rely on its assistance in helping him to achieve his objectives.

Having once received power, he then bathed as ritual purification in conjunction with other rites for a particular purpose. The power played an important role in compulsive magic—the performance of magic acts and prayer to produce a specific effect, such as to make whales drift ashore—and, again, its effectiveness lay in a perfectly correct performance of family-held secrets. The major rites were held by the head of the household in trust for the entire group, but certain people owned those connected with their fields of specialization. The hunter owned hunting rituals; the canoe-maker's guarded against the sun drying out and splitting the hull; the woodworker's helped him split straight planks out of a cedar log. Although many of these were hereditary and had originally been given to an ancestor, they differed from totem powers in that they had to be invoked.

Associated with these magic acts, but also used separately and on other occasions, were amulets and charms which had magic qualities and were kept for good luck. These were tufts of feathers or hair, and sometimes small incised stones, which were tied to weapons, worn around the neck, and carried in canoes. They were frequently exchanged between friends. Other similar charms had evil worked on them, and these would be secreted in a rival's canoe in an attempt to precipitate a disaster and bring misfortune. The Tlingit were so anxious about these that they always washed their canoes out before undertaking a long voyage. Various specialized amulets were believed to give assistance during events such as childbirth, puberty, menstruation, war, sickness, and when gambling.

A limited number of people were inspired by stronger spirit powers than others. These were the shamans. They formed an élite since the numbers of men and women with shamanistic abilities were very small, and they were sometimes considered as outsiders to the community— Tlingit shamans even had separate houses and were buried away from the villages. Their services were sought to predict the future and influence events in all the major crises of a person's life—for curing, hunting, war, rivalry, love and sorcery.

Their power was also obtained through a spirit-quest and ritual bathing, although this was carried out with greater intensity and more

Above : During curing rites Tsimshian shamans used small bone charms and amulets to represent the creatures from which they derived their powers. A bird, possibly a crane, is portrayed in this charm. A humanoid figure forms the bird's backbone with his head doubling as the bird's tail, while a moon-like face represents the wing joint. Intertwined elements with dual meanings and the use of figures to show joints, frequently symbolized by an eye shape, occur in many examples of northwest coast art.
Right : The Haida shaman wore a neck ring from which his various charms were suspended, and this generally had a wood or bone headscratcher and bone nose pins attached to it. The pointed cylindrical pendants here have been made by reworking a set of gambling sticks.

determination than for non-shamans. Often families had a tradition of shamanism as shamanistic parents would influence their children. Their power depended on the type of spirit they had contacted, and those giving this type of power were limited in number. For example, the Double-Headed Monster, Thunderbird, Land Otter and Fire were the only ones inspiring Salish shamans, and the Canoe-People, Ocean-People, Forest-People and Above-People were the only important ones amongst the Haida. Both groups, however, had numerous other spirits which conferred powers of a less specialized nature.

Since these forces were far stronger than, say, those of the canoe-maker or hunter, it was essential that an inexperienced novice who was unaccustomed to handling them underwent a training period. This might

Above : Theatrical art was highly developed on the coast with dramatic performances often enhanced through the use of elaborate stage properties. Puppets such as this featured in dance performances and curing ceremonies. They were often decorated with mica flakes to make their sudden arrival more spectacular, and had articulated joints which permitted them to move when hidden strings or rods were manipulated.

Right : A Tsimshian shaman may well have appeared before his patient dressed in this manner. He would tap the carved staff on the ground to warn of his approach, and accompanied his song with the rattle he is holding in his left hand. His crown is made from twenty-two grizzly-bear claws and a soul-catcher charm is attached to the end of the beaded necklace he is wearing.

last several years: the Salish remained secluded for four years, and saw only other shamans, before they were considered capable of using the power correctly. Kwakwabalas, a Kwakiutl, had to perform a dance for four successive winters before he could practise as a shaman, and he was made to observe certain conditions, including carving new masks for each performance and burning the old ones, before his powers became effective. During this training period the novice might be supervised and helped by one or more full shamans, who would 'sing over' him to fix his powers in order to prevent him from losing them or being possessed by them.

At the conclusion of his training a feast was given for him by his relatives during which his status as a full shaman was publicly announced. At this he was introduced to the group which would require his services. In some tribes the feast also served to ensure that his identity was known, as was necessary where shamans wore no special insignia except when performing a cure or some other shamanistic duty. In other tribes, however, they wore their hair dressed in a certain way or carried charms which singled them out.

Most had powers for curing and would be asked to help in cases of serious illness; generally these were cases in which the family's herbal remedies and own magic had proved ineffective. His role was similar to that of the modern psychotherapist since he was rarely, if ever, called on to cure physical ills, unless the patient was obviously very close to death.

Diagnosis and treatment were considered separately, and some shamans specialized in one or the other. The cause of the illness would be either the result of a malignant spirit force or the effect of sorcery, when it would stem from a disease object. These were small charms, usually two splinters of bone tied together with a hair, which were believed to have been sent into the patient's body by someone wishing him ill.

They were located by feeling over the patient's body, or by going into a trance when the shaman could 'see' through him as though he were transparent. He then pronounced the cause of the illness, stated whether or not a cure was possible and, if it was outside his own powers, possibly named someone who would be capable of performing it. The curing method differed according to the nature of the illness and which supernatural powers were being asked to give their assistance. Since shamanism was individual, each cure had its peculiarities, but they nearly always involved a trance, the removal and 'sending away' or 'killing' of the disease with the aid of spirits, and payment.

The patient's relatives would be present during the curing rite. A typical cure using elements from northern shamanistic practice might be as follows. Strewn about the floor, in a seemingly haphazard but carefully arranged order, lay symbols given by the shaman's spirits: a jointed puppet, a skull, a length of braided cedar bark or a small box containing shark's teeth and oddly shaped pebbles. The shaman crossed to the bed, his blackened face glistening in the flicker of the fire, and his hair twisted and coiled into long, matted plaits beneath a headdress of grizzly-bear claws.

A helper, perhaps the shaman's wife, beat a monotonous rhythm on a large box drum in time with the rattle that accompanied a slow song being hummed by the shaman. The humming was quiet and it was obvious that he was having difficulty in contacting his spirit powers. Some of the sick man's relatives placed a pile of blankets in the corner of the room, theoretically as payment to the shaman's spirits for their services (although most of these went eventually to the household heads and were used in potlatching). The humming grew louder as the spirits began to appear—visible only to the shaman who saw them standing around the sides of the house.

More goods were piled up and then the shaman began to sing, asking his powers for their assistance:

'I beg you, Supernatural Power, that you take pity and make well this our friend.

I implore you, Supernatural Power, that you take pity and take out this sickness of this our friend, Supernatural Power.

Oh, take pity that I may make alive this our friend, O Supernatural Power, that I may cure this our friend you go through, Supernatural Power.

That I may obtain easily this sickness of this our friend, O Great Real Supernatural Power, you Great Life-Bringer, Supernatural Power.' (Boas *Ethnology* p. 1295.)

The hypnotic beat of the drum continued and he went into a trance state, at the same time singing a healing song:

'Try to make him go through [the whole ceremonial], giver of the power of going through, Supernatural One.

Try to make him pure all through, giver of purity, Supernatural One.

I shall not do harm to you. I shall restore you to life, Supernatural One.

Pray, bring life to our friend, you supernatural life-bringer, who has gone through, Supernatural One.' (Boas *Ethnology* p. 1296.)

He then began to remove the disease object. If it was close to the surface he would be able to suck it out through a bone tube, but deeper objects had to be massaged out and removed by hand. As soon as he grasped the charm, he was thrown backwards by the force of its power, almost throwing off their balance two attendants who held on to his wide belt. A violent struggle ensued in which he pitted the strength of his own powers against those causing the illness. His attendants strained to prevent him from being flung completely out of the house, until at last he was able to quieten the spirit.

Showing the object to his audience, or displaying a ball of eagle down soaked in blood as a symbol of it, he asked them what they wanted him to do with it. He could 'send it away' by blowing it out of the smoke-hole, when it might return to the person responsible for sending it—among some tribes this would kill the sender, but in others it had no effect on him—or he was able to 'kill' it by throwing it into the fire.

It had, of course, been concealed about the shaman's person previous to its extraction, but this was not considered fraudulent. The shaman held that the spirits had told him to make it visible in this manner and, since it was done at their bidding, the trick itself was supernatural. However, a shaman might seek to expose the sleight of hand involved in an opponent's tricks, who was held to die of shame if exposed in this way.

A shaman's power was related to how effective his control over the spirits proved to be; therefore, he could not afford to fail in his cures too frequently. He might avoid criticism by diagnosing an illness as beyond cure, exclaiming that it was a pity the dying man's relatives had not called on him earlier before the spirits had taken such strong possession. At their urging he would attempt a cure, having absolved himself of blame if the patient died but increasing his prestige if the cure was a success since he had rescued someone from the brink of death.

Failure to perform effective cures was one of the main reasons for missionaries being able to undermine the authority of the shamans. Smallpox had preceded the arrival of the priests, and the shamans' powers had proved unable to prevent it spreading. This was in spite of their attempts at foretelling its incidence, naming who would be affected, and placing sacred markers around houses to ward off the evil. The missionaries, on the other hand, had vaccines with them. Their successful use of these so discredited the shamans that they ceased to be an in-fluential force and were unable to rouse opposition against these new adversaries.

Although curing was one of the most important functions of shaman-ism, and also a very dramatic one, it was by no means its only role. Shamanistic assistance was always required in cases of soul loss. The soul was believed to leave the body at night, when it travelled into the

Left : This Tlingit mask represents the face of an old woman's spirit and was probably worn by a shaman during curing rites, since it was found in a shaman's grave-house near Yakutat. The woman's lower lip is pushed forward by a labret, or lip-plug. Only high-status women had the right to wear a labret, the size of which was increased as they aged; this woman must have enjoyed both high status and advanced years. Facial painting is shown to indicate her crest affiliation.
Above : Inlaid and incised soul-catchers were the most important items used by curing shamans. When sickness was believed to be the result of the soul leaving the body, a shaman could be hired to search for the errant soul which he enticed to enter the soul-catcher. With the apertures at either end securely plugged with cedar bark stoppers, the soul could be safely carried back to the patient and restored. The soul-catcher shown here was used by a Tsimshian shaman.

Other World, from which dreams originated. Usually it returned before dawn, but it could travel so far that it was unable to return in time; or it might be stolen by the spirits, particularly those of the seas, or by a shaman who had been paid to do so by a rival. An errant soul could be returned by using a soul-catcher: an ivory or bone amulet which had two apertures into which the soul might be received. It was believed that it was actually swallowed by the catcher and that the shaman had to retrieve it in order to restore it to his patient.

Some powerful shamans had the ability to travel to the Other World in search of wandering souls. Painted boards representing a spirit canoe were erected by the Salish, and a pantomime journey was made in them to the Land of the Dead. In contrast, Nootkan shamans set out physically on their search. A line was attached around the shaman's waist so that he would be able to find his way back, and he was then believed to journey under the sea. This was performed at night and out of sight of the patient's relatives, who were required to remain in the house. He followed the tracks left by the soul, while his attendants waited on the beach and tied on additional lengths of line as his journey took him further away. On returning, he would be dripping wet and streaming with blood, carefully carrying a symbolic soul (a ball of eagle down) in his cupped hands.

Soul loss did not mean immediate death but an extremely prolonged process of increasing lassitude. Frequently a person did not even know he was suffering from it until a shaman noticed it and told him. It was important that the soul should be recovered as quickly as possible, and the further it wandered then the more difficult, and costly, a cure became. If it reached the Land-of-the-Forever-Dead it was irretrievable, making eventual death a certainty and preventing the person from being reincarnated.

Sometimes, especially when cures became protracted, the shaman might be accused of being guilty of the theft in order to earn a curing fee. It was quite generally believed that a person with the ability to find souls could also steal them, and that someone who removed disease objects also had the power to send them. If he was discovered using his powers in this way it was explained that he had been compelled to do so by his spirits. Belief in the shaman's domination of his spirits was reconciled with this power of theirs to make him act against his will by the supposition that he did not have total domination but could only ask their assistance, and that the spirits had negative forces which could not be entirely suppressed.

Spirit possession was another area in which a shaman's help was necessary, but so serious was this that even he could only be of any assistance if the possession was incomplete. A spirit would be seen clinging to its victim's back 'as though there were two of him there', and the shaman would set his own forces against those afflicting his patient. Dislodging this possessive force required considerable supernatural strength and very few shamans would even attempt a cure. If they did so, and the spirit in question was a shamanistic one, they might try to gain it themselves, as the acquisition of additional sources of supernatural help elevated status.

Shamans were just as conscious of their status as the rest of north-west coast Indian society. Two opposing shamans of high social position would pit their powers against each other in a 'battle' in order to gain the prestige that victory would bring. When one of them decided that his spirits had 'killed' those of his rival, he would invite other shamans to 'feast on his enemy's bones'. Since they did not have this type of supernatural vision laymen were unable to see the 'bones' and received the impression that they were witnessing a pantomime meal. Meanwhile, the 'dead' rival would be searching, supernaturally, for his 'bones' so that they could be restored. Without them he was spiritually dead and physical death was certain to follow. Another form of destroying a

Left: A Haida shaman's rattle carved with the design of a killer-whale. A small killer-whale face may be seen in the mouth of the larger head; a sea-monster face is carved on the reverse side. Rattles of this type were made in two halves which were bound or sewn together after 'noisemakers' had been placed inside – this rattle contains nine small pebbles.

Above: The 'Amhalayt', or chief's ceremonial headdress, was the most essential part of the regalia worn during a Tsimshian potlatch, since it was closely associated with the supernatural creatures from whom the chief obtained his power. Only the finest artists were commissioned to make them. This one has a particularly well-balanced design: the large central face is set in a rectangular border of abalone, and attention is drawn to it by the double row of monstrous heads and single row of heads with bodies which surround the border.

rival was 'naming to death', which undermined a rival's position by using his name instead of the words for food and drink: 'Give me some [rival's name] to drink, I'm thirsty!'

This same type of 'battle' was also an important element in warfare. Shamans of opposing tribes would harangue each other and insult the other's spiritual helpers. Quite frequently this resulted in one of them deciding that his powers were inferior, and he would go off to seek additional ones. This marked the end of the battle, which had happened without coming to physical conflict. David Samwell, the surgeon travelling with Captain Cook, describes one such Nootkan engagement:

Far left : Although similar in concept to a Chilkat dance apron, this Tlingit shaman's apron has painted visionary symbols instead of the dance apron's woven crest designs. Here the painted areas are outlined with embroidery, and porcupine quillwork is used to reiterate the apron's basic shape. Quillwork reflects an influence from the Tlingit's Athabascan neighbours, with whom they had extensive trade contact.

Left : Four days after a shaman's death his body was stuffed into a grave box which had lines of operculum inlay decorating the lid. This was placed in a small shelter overlooking water and away from the village. His spirits were believed to remain close to the body and prevent its decay ; consequently, the Tlingit generally kept away from the place and made an offering whenever a canoe passed within sight of one of these shelters. There was, so it is said, one exception to the rule of avoidance : when a would-be shaman was unable to contact a spirit, he could visit the grave and remove one of the dead shaman's teeth. By holding this grisly trophy in his mouth he was certain to contact one of the spirits formerly controlled by the deceased.

'After the canoes had come within a prudent distance of their opponents they lay upon their paddles, when a Man started up in a violent fury on shore & advancing with his Spear in his Hand to the Water's Edge, made a long Speech, sputtering his words out with the utmost Vehemence & throwing out Saliva from his Mouth, seemingly in the most violent Rage and agitation of mind, to which the motions of his Body corresponded which were violent to an extream—in short his whole actions were those of a man out of his Senses. After continuing reviling his Enemies in this manner for some minutes or till he was tired he went back to his party & sat down among them as composed as if nothing had happened. During the time he was making his Speech the adverse party were quite silent, but as soon as he had done a Man started up among them & using the same violent Actions and Gestures as the other had done returned the obloqy & Abuse, & thus they continued reviling each other for several Hours till at last the grand fleet paddled out of the Cove.' (Samwell's *Journal*, 4 April 1778.)

As the forces that the shaman claimed to control were outside the understanding of normal people—a situation deliberately encouraged by the secrecy and mysticism surrounding shamanistic ritual—there was a tendency to view the shamans with some degree of suspicion. This was directed at the possibility that they might be guilty of mal-practice, rather than fraud. It was possible to hire a shaman to work evil magic. Even though few of them cared to admit that they did so, most people thought that they could if they wished. Some, whose powers

Right: Commemorative carving representing Owl-Man; Tlingit, from Yakutat. According to the legend, Owl-Man was killed at Icy Bay about 1890 by a tree which fell on him, and the body was only found because hordes of crows were picking at it. The carving shows him with a bird's body and a human head; the base represents a crow. It is believed to have been carved from the tree which killed him and was used at feasts which honoured his memory.

Far right: A Haida shaman wandered alone into the woods where he had an accident and broke both his legs. Unable to return to the village for assistance he starved to death, and his emaciated body was not found until some time later. This carving was made and suspended at the grave site to commemorate the event. His feet point downward in the position they would occupy if the figure reclined.

were so strong that they could resist any possible retaliation, might admit that they practised such powers and were greatly feared.

Even more feared were the sorcerers, since these were ordinary people who had been possessed by an evil force which they were unable to control. They could as easily be the neighbour's four-year-old daughter as an old grandfather, and it was impossible to identify them unless they were caught in the act of performing one of their rituals. Since their powers compulsively passed down through generations, entire families came under suspicion if one relative were found guilty, although not all members would have been contaminated. A sorcerer was killed immediately his or her identity was known, usually by members of the same kin or clan group, and possibly close relatives would suffer the same fate. As a result, sorcerers were very careful to hide their identities.

The spells they cast caused anything from minor irritation to misfortune, abnormal behaviour and death. People who lied or stole, for example, were considered the victims of sorcery. They could only be cured by undoing the spell, but since this required knowledge of its whereabouts, which depended on knowing the sorcerer's identity, it was rarely possible. Magic was worked on something personal from the intended victim—a fragment of clothing perhaps, a lock of hair, an intangible such as breath, or, commonly, excrement. Incantations were performed over this, and perhaps some magic herbs were sprinkled on it or a charm of some sort tied around it, and it was then placed in contact with a corpse. Anyone seen in the vicinity of a shaman's grave at night would be immediately suspected of sorcery, as the remnants of shamanistic power rendered a sorcerer's spell especially potent. The graves most frequently visited were those of the recent dead. The sorcerer was thought capable of changing from his human form when visiting graves, and many Tsimshian tales tell of dogs being killed at graveyards in the belief that they were disguised sorcerers. New graves were usually guarded by the deceased's relatives for a ritual period of four days, after which the soul left the body, to prevent their being used in witchcraft.

If a person thought he might have been bewitched, he would attempt to ascertain the identity of the person he believed was guilty. Some shamans, twins in particular since they had the power of clairvoyance, might be able to establish this. Alternatively, he could appeal to the spirits of the trees to reveal it during a dream:

'Oh, friends, turn your faces to me, look through me, Supernatural Ones, because I have been bewitched, that I may die. I have come, Supernatural Ones, to beg you to take pity on me and to try to save my life, that I may live. Listen to me. I beg your help, Supernatural Ones, O Life-Bringers, Supernatural Ones, and this is what I ask of you, Supernatural Ones, that you may take away the power of witchcraft against me, Supernatural Ones, you to whom nothing is impossible, Supernatural Ones. I mean that you will let me dream a good dream this night.' (Boas *Ethnology* p. 1327.)

Sometimes a sorcerer received punishment by unwittingly working magic against himself. A young man who was quite wealthy and had several jealous rivals woke up during the night to find a long pole, with cedar bark wrapped around the end, being poked through a knot hole in the house planking and held under his nose. He pretended to be asleep, but looked through the knot hole when the pole was withdrawn and recognized the person who had been holding it. By making another similar pole, holding this under the sorcerer's nose, and then changing the poles over, he made the sorcerer work the magic on himself and 'steal his own breath'. Some time later, when he was out swimming, he suddenly began gasping for air and drowned.

Anyone who died in such a dishonourable way went to the sky and meteors were believed to be the stones dropping down from their funeral pyres. The Tsimshian, in common with other northern tribes, associated the aurora borealis with murderers who were burning up as they tried to return to earth. 'Murder' here meant supernatural killing and witchcraft; actual murders were rare and revenge killings in feuds were not considered as such.

Some groups, particularly the Salish and Kwakiutl, had such an exaggerated belief in the powers of sorcery that they no longer believed anyone died from natural causes, but that all deaths were the result of magic or spirits. Even an obvious accident, such as slipping and falling from a cliff, was explained by assuming that the person had been pushed over by a spirit.

Most people went to the lower world at death, although they maintained close spiritual contact with their living relatives. This contact was made stronger by the belief that they would be reincarnated after a ritual period of four years. On his deathbed, a Kwakiutl might take leave of his friends and promise to return to them again soon:

'Farewell, O friends! for I am leaving you, O friends!
    Farewell, O brothers! for I am leaving you, O brothers!
    O friends! do not take it too much to heart that I am leaving you, O friends!
    O brothers! do not take it too much to heart that I am leaving you, O brothers!
    O sisters! do not feel too sorrowful because I am leaving you, O sisters!
    I was told by the one who takes care of me that I shall not stay away long, that I shall come back to you, O friends!
    I mean, O friends! that you shall not feel too sorrowful when I leave you, O friends!' (Boas *Ethnology* p. 1307.)

Myth and Cosmology

The traditional beliefs and legends of the northwest coast constituted a complex and very full mythology. Under the title of myth are included all those stories which deal with the origin of man and his customs, and which are concerned with supernatural contacts and occurrences. Since the Indian was fond of rhetoric, stories were creatively embellished by numerous asides explaining the nature of the fabulous beings, often accompanied by a change in the tenor of the story-teller's voice to indicate the different characters. These gave the tales an entertainment and amusement value additional to their semi-historical function of defining traditions.

They spoke of happenings from mythological time—a period which was 'long ago', although how long was usually rather indeterminate since they were simply tales from the past which explained the condition of the present.

Unlike most societies the northwest coast Indians did not have creation myths and even their tales depicting earliest events assumed that a world was already in existence, although it may have been covered with water and perpetually dark. Nor was there a Creator figure of any description except for a rather vaguely defined Chief-Above who lived in a house in the sky and exercised some control over man's destiny, but it is very likely that this personage did not feature in mythology until after the advent of Christianity. An abundance of stories, however, dealt with the origins of natural phenomena—particular mountains or islands, thunderstorms, or the growth of trees—or explained the transformation of elements, such as the development of rough tree bark from originally smooth trees or the way an animal gained dark coloration through being scorched by the sun.

Central to the origin and transformation stories were the Original People. They occupied the world at the beginning of time, although not necessarily in human form. Since the people and animals living in the real world developed from these Original People, tales refer to tribes which consisted of, say, Raven, Mink, Otter and Porpoise-Woman, or to 'people' called Sun, Moon and Star. These were all myth-creatures with human characteristics whose behaviour bore as much resemblance to the human world as to that of the animals: no one would expect a real eagle to behave in the same manner as the mythological Eagle, but they might share characteristics such as keen eyesight or the ability to fly very high. Living in houses, they performed the same daily chores as man and had many customs which were later exclusive to humans.

In this Quileute (Coast Salish) myth, which explains the origin of the stars, the human-animal nature of the Original People is expressed quite clearly. In common with many other myths, the world is put into order through acts which are incidental to the main theme— Whale, Porpoise and Wren all find their correct places more or less accidentally, and Eagle gains his sharp eyesight at Snail's expense. It begins with a potlatch:

'In the long ago, when all things were human beings, Whale was the biggest person then as he is the largest animal now. His daughter, Miss Porpoise, had just been admitted into the Tsayik Dance Society, and he was going to give a great Potlatch in her honour.'

Various contests were held for the amusement of the guests before the potlatch began:

'Whale himself arrived, carrying a large yew-wood bow which was greater in length than any tree now growing. Its bowstring was twisted whale intestines, and the arrow he carried to be used with the bow was many, many paces in length.'

He threw this down and challenged his guests to shoot it, offering his daughter's hand in marriage as the prize. Neither Bear nor Cougar was able to accomplish this, but Wren called on his Guardian Spirit and was successful, shooting the arrow so high that it was lost from sight.

'Suddenly it was discovered that Snail had not attended the potlatch. Furthermore, it was known that he had very penetrating, powerful eyes. So Eagle was sent to bring him to the place of the meeting. Now Eagle was always a thief as now, so, finding Snail asleep, he plucked out his eyes and appropriated them himself. That's why Eagle has such sharp eyes and Snail has none; Eagle is using Snail's eyes even in our own time.'

With the aid of Snail's eyes, Eagle showed Wren the arrow sticking in the sky. Wren shot further arrows skywards, shooting each into the notch of the previous one, until a chain of them reached all the way back to earth. The people then climbed hand over hand up this chain until they entered the Sky-World where they camped by a large river.

Right : The Skeena River valley, through which the Tsimshian's ancestors are believed to have travelled from the legendary Temlaxam, to escape privation in the subarctic interior.

'When our people camped there, it was very cold; but across the river they could see a fire. So Mink swam over and stole a few gleaming coals, put them in his rain hat and recrossed the river with them; but his act was discovered before he had hardly crossed to the side of the people of earth.

Instantly the heavenly war whoop could be heard on every side. The river soon swarmed with canoes and in an incredibly short time a terrible battle was on. The people of the earth were defeated and soon were trying to climb down the ladder in panic order; but the worst was to come. Before half of them were down, the ladder became unjointed and fell to earth, crushing all who were on it, and the other unfortunates are still up there in the starry vault, for they have never yet been able to get down to their old home.

After the ladder fell there was great trouble in Whale's house. Cougar blamed Whale and Wren for all the trouble, and soon a fight was on. Cougar scratched Whale on his lower jaw and caused great slits, alternating with ridges, to be formed. You can see them on Whale's chin and breast to this day. Finally, to escape with his life, Whale took to the sea with his daughter, Miss Porpoise, where they have lived ever since. At the same time Wren, who was also very much scared, made his body so small that he escaped through a knot hole in the lodge. Then to the brush he betook himself for protection and has been a small, skulking-about fellow ever since.

The people of earth who were still up above when the ladder became disjointed are there still. Some were made stars. Others were more powerful than their neighbours and now are ruling chiefs in their own respective sections, but none have ever been able to get back to earth. The great snake [the Milky Way] which encircles the dark sky, Big Elk and Little Elk [Big and Little Dippers], Cougar, Bear, the Smelt Dip Net, Whale's Chair [Cassiopeia], Skate, Salmon, Wren's Meat Tray [Delphinus], these and many more, you can see any clear night. Rainbow is also still up there. We see it in the daytime. As you know, it is a huge bird; and the bright coloured arches we see are its legs. Its feet are armed with powerful talons with which it often seizes firm hold upon the earth; but its large body, the clouds, is in the sky, and though it often struggles hard, it cannot draw itself down to earth by its gripping feet. In the long ago after this rainbow became one of the heavenly hosts, it also gave birth to a child, a daughter of one of the children of earth, and every now and then, the mother comes forth with her child, the secondary rainbow, and scours the earth to see if she can see her child's father; but to this time she has never seen him since that unfortunate day. Then, because she cannot find him, she and her daughter meet and cry. You can hear their voices in the mournful wind; the rain is their tears.' (Jay Powell and Vickie Jensen *Quileute: an introduction to the Indians of La Push* p. 47.)

A complete cycle of myths concerns the transformation of the world. These are the Trickster tales. They concern a character whose inquisitive nature and constant bragging are always getting him into trouble. Although he usually manages to escape any serious consequences, during his attempts to extricate himself from these difficulties he alters features of nature. The elements contained in this cycle of myths are found throughout the northwest coast, and have parallels over much of the American continent, so that similar stories occur among all the groups with only minor changes in detail.

Trickster was called Raven by the Tlingit, Tsimshian and Haida. It is probable that the myths originated in this area, since the cycle is most complete here, and then spread south where Raven has his counterparts in the forms of Mink and Bluejay. Because Raven was the original Trickster his stories tend to be truer to type than those of the southern groups, although all are frequently connected with the Original People.

Typical of the Raven tales are those in which he stole fresh water but in his hurry to escape spilt drops, thus forming the rivers and lakes. In another example he tricked Seagull into giving him eulachon and then pretended he had caught them in a river. This angered the chief who owned them, and he accidentally released all the fish when he went to check the trap beneath his house. Raven obtained fire by disguising himself as a deer and setting his tail alight. When the owner of fire pursued him he hid among the trees, which began to burn, and since then people have been able to use fire.

The benefits he conferred by stealing water, fish and fire from the three chiefs who owned them were obviously of tremendous use to man, but this was not Raven's motive. His interest was in satisfying his own desires and it was only by chance that the changes he caused were

Worn as crest headdresses, Tsimshian sun masks were usually carved on an almost flat plane and had projections which represented the sun's rays. On this example, the projections are painted with sea-monster designs. The large, flat area of the mask reflected the light from the fire as the dancer moved, giving an impression of a glowing sun face.

helpful. In many ways he was a daredevil, although he often resorted to trickery, and the thefts proved he could achieve success against more powerful adversaries. His craftiness is shown in his theft of the sun, one of the most widespread of the Raven myths, which also shows how he could change his form at will, even assuming human form.

He had become bored—another of his characteristics—at living in a world of darkness (the sun was kept in the Sky-World) and therefore resolved to visit the home of the Sky-Chief and steal the box which contained the sun. He made a hole in the clouds through which he entered this Other World, then changed himself into a leaf floating in a container of water. Sky-Chief's daughter swallowed this when she took a drink and consequently became pregnant. (Pregnancy caused by swallowing a leaf, sometimes a twig or a pine needle, is a common myth theme.) Her baby boy, who was really Raven, was continually pleading for the box until the chief gave it to him to play with. Resuming his normal shape, Raven flew out of the smoke-hole with the box and returned to earth.

Below : A view on the Queen Charlotte Islands. Having been banished from his sky home at a time when the world was still covered with water, Raven became tired from flying but could find no resting place. He created the islands for this purpose by dropping stones he carried with him or, alternatively, by splashing the water with his wings and transforming the spray to rock.
Right : A Tsimshian whalebone knife hilt depicting Raven. The very refined sense of shape apparent in this carving shows the skill for which Tsimshian carvers were justly acclaimed.

He felt very hungry and wandered about for some time looking for food. A group of fishermen he met refused to give him anything to eat, but an old chief pitied him and gave him some eulachon. Raven told him to close his eyes because he was going to open the box. When he did this the world became light and those who had allowed him to go hungry were turned into frogs. In some other tales the fishermen were really ghosts who vanished when the box was opened, as a result of which ghosts now live in dark regions and only visit man's world at night.

The hunger he feels in this story is a feature of many Raven myths. In fact, extreme greed is very characteristic of all the Trickster figures, and it is often on account of his inability to prevent himself from stealing food that he gets into difficult situations. According to Tsimshian myths, Raven only became greedy as the result of a trick played on him by a slave called Mouth-at-Each-End; he then ate all the tribe's provisions and was thrown out since he was threatening them with starvation.

In examples from some other tales his greed is very apparent. In one he tried to drown a fisherman so that he could eat all his catch. However, the fisherman was half-halibut and swam back, catching Raven and giving him a severe beating. On another occasion Crow had asked him to cure her child since Raven had some shamanistic power. He sent her out to fetch water, but while she was away he stole the seal she had caught. When he was fishing with Cormorant, he suggested that, since Cormorant was not catching many fish, he should cut his tongue and use the blood as bait. Cormorant did so and caught a great deal, which Raven then claimed as his own, and since Cormorant's tongue was hurt, he was unable to speak and could not argue. At a feast he left excrement outside the feast house and instructed it to shout 'Crowds of warriors'. When it did the occupants rushed out to defend the village, leaving Raven behind to eat all the food.

Nevertheless, his tricks were frequently unsuccessful and at times he appears rather foolish and naive. This gives the impression that he had somewhat of a dual character: very clever at one moment, especially when trying to find a way out of a tight corner, but incredibly gullible on other occasions. For instance, when Bear invited him for a meal he was served grease, which Bear obtained by holding his hands above the fire and letting it drip from his fingers. When Raven attempted the same, his fingers shrivelled up and turned black.

This same myth appears in the south with Bluejay as the protagonist, where Sea-Lion issued the invitation and cut him a slice of blubber from his own side. When Bluejay invited Sea-Lion back he tried to imitate this and wounded himself so severely that he was almost killed. Upon his recovery, Bluejay visited Seal and was given Seal's youngest son to eat. The boy came back to life, but Bluejay's own son remained dead when he copied this trick.

Bluejay does not transform himself as much as Raven, relying instead on the tricks he plays on people, such as convincing them that he is one of five identical brothers so that he can eat five times. In another tale he challenges Seal to see who could stay underwater longest. Bluejay only pretended to dive, and hid himself under some floating brush. Seal waited so long for a signal that he had won that he drowned.

The third Trickster, Mink, has the qualities of Raven and Bluejay but the myths about him often have a strong erotic element. He spends much of his time in planning ways of tricking his own daughters and seducing those of other people, and many of his stories were censored when Europeans collected them. It is said that the Indians, who were hardly puritanical, only told erotic Mink tales to the boys. In practice, the girls could hear them too since they sat close by—but they were told not to listen!

Trickster is often held responsible for the absolute nature of death, although this may also be credited to Wren since he built his house beneath grave-boxes in the days when they were hung in trees. In the

Raven myths, Raven told Eagle, whose son had died, that the dead should remain dead. He repented when his own son died but was unable to reverse the decision. And in the following Bluejay story the dead are prevented from returning to this world through the disrespect he shows when he visits the Land of the Dead.

Bluejay's sister had married a dead person and he decided to visit her. Although he thought that the Land of the Dead was on the other side of a wide river, there was no reply when he called, and, since he had travelled all day, he began to yawn. Because the dead could hear yawns but not shouts they sent an empty canoe across. Bluejay saw that it was a burial canoe, for it had holes drilled through the bottom to allow rain-water to drain off, but his sister's voice reassured him and he climbed in. There were some old bones in the canoe, which he threw into the river. On reaching the opposite shore he was scolded by his sister for almost drowning his brother-in-law, and everywhere he looked there were bones and skulls, which Bluejay kicked out of his path. Since these were really dead people he annoyed everyone considerably, and when his behaviour failed to improve they asked him to leave.

A warning was given for his return journey that he would have to cross five burning prairies for which he was allowed five containers of water. The smallest container was meant for the first prairie but Blue-jay ignored the advice and used the largest, so by the time he reached the fifth he had very little water left. This ran out when he was halfway across and he burnt to death. Suddenly he was back at the river where a man in a magnificent canoe waited to take him to the village, which was full of people. Since that day, only shamans with the power to recover lost souls can go to the Land of the Dead and return.

The Land of the Dead is regularly depicted, as here, as being near to the world of the living, even though there is no return. There are direct connections with it *via* house fires and grave sites, and some animals and birds, particularly owls, are thought to be dead souls. The Sky-Worlds are also close, just beyond the clouds, and are reached in the myths by the arrow chain, by a ladder reaching to the stars, by a rope let down by Spider-Woman, and by the Rainbow. Earth, sea and sky are joined by mountainous islands which, on this section of the coast, rise straight up from the water and have their peaks wreathed in clouds.

The Indians' view of the worlds of the living and the dead was quite self-contained. They had no need, nor desire, to speculate about lands far across the oceans or deep in the cosmos. In fact, the Kwakiutl considered the ocean to be a wide river which ran to the north—the source of supernatural power and where Cannibal-at-the-North-End-of-the-World had his home. The same, almost homely, concern with only the immediate environment is shown by the numerous myths featuring animals which explain how they obtained their present form or describe their origin. Raven, for example, in one myth becomes black through sitting in the smoke-hole of a house; in another he waits until all the other birds have painted themselves, and then discovers that all the colours have been used and only black remains.

In a Bella Coola myth about a woman who married the Sun, there is an episode in which their child burnt all the Sun's torches at once and made the earth very hot, although he had been told to burn small ones in the morning and evening, and a large one at noon. Ermine tried to escape the heat by hiding beneath a rock, but the tip of his tail was showing and it was scorched black. Mountain Goat, on the other hand, hid in a cave and remained completely white. A very common tale, known to most of the groups, explains the creation of mosquitoes from the ashes of a cannibal who was burnt by the youngest of five brothers in revenge for killing his family.

The myths do not just give the Original People human qualities; they also account for characteristics of animal behaviour. Deer and

Left : Bokwus, the Kwakiutl Wild-Man-of-the-Woods and chief of the dead. The skeletal Bokwus lived in an invisible house deep in the forests, where he subsisted on rotten wood and grubs— the food of ghosts. He offered what appeared to be dried salmon to people chancing upon him but, after tasting this, they died and joined his ghostly retinue.

Above : An item of Tsimshian stage-craft, this wooden heart was hidden on a dancer who was thrown into the fire. He emerged wearing a skull-like mask but with his heart displayed intact ; the heart suddenly opened (bottom) to reveal an owl. Since owls were believed to be the souls of the recently dead, this may symbolize the dancer's spiritual death.

Right : Although catalogued as an 'ape-like face', this Tsimshian mask is almost certainly meant to appear like a skull and probably represents a corpse. It was used during the same series of dances as the wooden heart shown on the previous page.
Far right : A pencilled note on the reverse of this carving says 'Sitka 1810' which places it in Tlingit territory, but it is almost definitely made by the Haida. Described as 'a sea-monster carrying a woman on its back', the blunt nose and crescent-shaped gill-slits behind the eyes indicate that a dog-fish is actually represented. The nude figure of the woman is an uncommon feature in carvings of this nature ; however, her presence becomes clearer if the carving is related to a Haida myth from the village of Massett. This myth tells us that the dog-fish was first used as a crest after a woman was carried away by the Dog-Fish-People as a punishment for doing something that displeased them.

Wolf play laughing at each other, and when Wolf notices that Deer has no teeth he eats him. The Salish tell a story of Robin, in which Robin attempts to kill his wife, who goes underwater and becomes the Periwinkle. Regretting his action, he tries to persuade her to come back to him by singing his song in the early morning and evening. The mythical animals were often credited with supernatural powers: the ability of Killer-Whales to change themselves into Wolves, as in Nootkan myth, for example. They might use these to control some natural forces; Porcupine in this tale is able to make water freeze by singing:

'The Beaver and the Porcupine were great friends and went about everywhere together. The Porcupine often visited the Beaver's house, but the latter did not like to have him come because he left quills there. One time, when the Porcupine said that he wanted to go out to the Beaver's house, the Beaver said, "All right, I will take you out on my back." He started, but instead of going to his house he took him to a stump in the very middle of the lake. Then he said to him, "This is my house," left him there, and went ashore.

While the Porcupine was upon this stump he began singing a song, "Let it become frozen. Let it become frozen so that I can cross to Wolverine-Man's place." He meant that he wanted to walk ashore on the ice. So the surface of the lake froze, and he walked ashore.

Some time after this, when the two friends were again playing together, the Porcupine said, "You come now. It is my turn to carry you on my back." Then the Beaver got on the Porcupine's back, and the Porcupine took him to the top of a very high tree, after which he came down and left him. For a long time the Beaver did not know how to get down, but finally he climbed down, and they say that this is what gives the broken appearance to tree bark.' (Stith Thompson *Tales of the N. American Indians* p. 75.)

All the myths we have considered so far have been concerned with the Original People and/or animals, and most of them refer to a period before the people had separate identities as tribal or cultural units. Another type of legend explains the division into the many language groups: the flood stories. According to these the land was completely flooded at one time—and there is archaeological evidence that extensive floods did occur—when only the peaks of mountains remained above water. In their attempts to escape the rising tide the people took to canoes and became separated, eventually settling in different areas and forming the many divisions found on the coast. In Tlingit myth, everyone attempted to escape on a single large raft, which became stranded on a rock. Its weight broke the raft in two when the flood waters receded, and the Tlingit became separated from all the other people.

Many flood stories begin with a misunderstanding among the Original People. According to the Salish, the flood was caused when Thrush was forced to wash her face despite her warning that something disastrous would happen if she did so. As she washed the dirt off it began to rain, leaving streaks across her face which can be seen to this day. The rain continued for sixty days and nights. The Tlingit believed the flood was caused by Raven, who asked Tide-Woman to raise the waters so that he might look under the ocean. They believe that there are still the remains of rock walls which the Original People built to keep the waters at bay on the tops of the mountains which were used as refuges.

Another flood tale is a Haida one in which a jealous chief attempted to destroy his nephew who he thought was having an affair with his wife. He set about this by putting on a magical wooden hat which grew taller while water poured out of it. Raven also features in this story, since it was he who pushed the hat back down and broke it into wooden rings—which incidentally became the islands of Skidegate inlet.

Other tales describe the period after the flood. In these, people were living in an environment which was essentially the same as the present, although the events they describe still take place in mythological time. These are connected with the previous myths and had some shared motifs, which frequently overlap, making the time boundary between the groups indistinct. Included in them are tales in which a man carves a wooden image of an animal, usually of Whale or Seal, and brings it to life, and those where he obtains supernatural power by living in an animal household—often with the Salmon, who gives the power of rejuvenation.

The Nootkan Wolf myths belong with this group, and are some of the most important animal tales since they formed the basis for the Nootkan Winter Ceremonial, the Wolf Dance. In these a man meets the Wolves who demonstrate their powers of reviving the dead by singing magical songs. The person they bring back to life is human, but he is able to assume Wolf form by donning a Wolf coat. On the strength of this myth, the Nootka traditionally believed that dead men would be reincarnated as Wolves.

The superhuman qualities given to mythical people, such as those suggested in the Wolf story, are widely encountered and have many parallels. Marriages with animals occur frequently and are usually associated with the acquisition of special powers over the animal in question; Bear- and Dog-husband tales are widely distributed.

Bear-husband tales begin with the kidnapping of a woman who has insulted the Bears by expressing disgust after stepping in their excrement. The Bears take her to their home, where she breaks off small pieces from her copper bracelet and leaves these on the ground each time she relieves herself. This convinces them that their excrement really is disgusting in comparison with hers and her life is spared. She marries the Bear chief's son and has children who have human form in their own home but put on Bear coats when they go out. After living with the Bears for several years she is rescued by her brother, who kills the

Right : Detail from the Eagle and Beaver pole at Tanu, a Haida village south of Skedans. Standing 16m (52ft 9in) high, this was one of the tallest poles carved by the Haida. The detail shows a human figure who is holding a frog and which refers to Volcano-Woman ; her use on the pole is explained by the myth in which a young man threw a frog into the fire and killed it. When he did this, a voice called, 'O, give me back my child, my only child!' Only an old woman and her daughter took any notice ; they dug a pit in which they stored provisions and slept there each night. Soon after this the village was engulfed in smoke and fire, and only the old woman and her daughter, secure in their pit, were saved.

Right, below : Tsimshian Flying-Frog headpiece. Many flying frogs came out of a lake two years after the disappearance of the ancestress of a Frog clan. Following their appearance, a house front painting was seen floating on the water and on this sat the woman—her knees, breasts, eyebrows and the backs of her hands were covered with frogs. Since that time the Frog has been a special crest.

Far right : Many transformation masks were used by the northern tribes. They were opened at appropriate moments in the dance to reveal different aspects of the figure the dancer was impersonating. This Haida mask opens to reveal a human face, expressing the dual human/animal nature of the spirits.

Bear-husband, and the children, remaining human from now on, are able to kill bears with ease since they are related.

In the Dog-husband stories, a young woman's pet dog assumes human form at night and they have a sexual relationship, which results in her giving birth to five puppies. The tribe abandons her and hangs her husband, but Crow takes pity and leaves fire so that she will not be completely helpless. Each day she can hear children's voices coming from the house while she is out collecting food, so she looks through a crack in the house boards and sees the puppies in human form, with their Dog coats hanging on the wall. By burning the coats she forces her children to remain human. They discover that they have the power to obtain food easily, and when the tribe, who are suffering privation, return, they forgive her. The children grow up as chiefs.

Although in the above tales a person receives special powers over a particular species of animal through an association with it, they were not necessarily used to relate the origins of specific clans. Indeed, in the Bear-husband tales, the law of incest would compel the woman to marry into a clan opposite to the Bears', and since her children inherited clan affiliation from her, they, too, would be in an opposite group to that of the Bear. The clans had their own origin myths which are different from animal myths in general in that the clan stories were the property of the clan who owned the right to recite them, since they referred to the acquisition of exclusive supernatural powers.

Clan myths merge almost imperceptibly with Hero stories, a group of tales centred on the exploits of humans who overcome supernatural forces. Some of them belonged to the community, while others were the property of certain lineages. The latter traced history as a sequence of mythical events, which were sometimes based on fact. They were jealously guarded, and their precise significance was often known only to their owners.

Hero stories feature characters such as Stone-Ribs or Lazy Boy who search out and destroy forces which threaten the tribe's existence. Stone-Ribs can do so because his body is almost entirely of stone and he is, therefore, practically invulnerable. The Lazy Boy myth concerns a person who is always sleeping and is the butt of the tribe's taunts. But when danger threatens in the form of an onrushing forest which is pushing the village into the sea he wakes up and demonstrates his tremendous strength by pushing the forest back out of harm's way. After several similar adventures he leaves to replace his grandfather in the job of holding the world up on a long pole, teaching people the moral that they should never ridicule someone they do not know.

Other Hero stories tell of visits to other worlds and the contests which have to be won. They may involve, for example, the Sun's testing of his son-in-law (who is human) by challenging him to perform feats such as producing fresh berries in winter or killing dangerous animals with soft arrow points. Or they pit him against the impossible odds of far superior forces like Whirpool, North Wind and Ice.

Even though the origin stories recited during the Winter Ceremonials were quite similar to these Hero tales, the religious aspect of myth was of a secondary nature. Far more emphasis was placed on the importance of mythology in explaining man's place in the world and in affirming traditional customs. During the long, cool winter evenings, the children gathered about the fires to listen to their grandfathers telling them the stories of where light came from and how the lakes were formed; of Raven, Lazy Boy, Deer or Porcupine; and of how their great-great-grandfather had spent months searching for the Bears who had stolen his sister. Thus, every child grew up with an understanding of the ways in which the world, man and the animals were created, and with a knowledge of the exploits of supernatural beings and their mythical ancestors.

Dance and Ceremony

Throughout the ages, from the earliest subsistence cultures up to and including our own civilization, man has attempted to establish order in his world by assigning various roles to unseen forces and divine powers. Conduct and ritual which are designed to influence these powers or are devoted to them may be defined as 'religion'. Although no northwest coast language contains any word which translates as such—since the coast Indians considered secular and religious life as inseparable and did not make this distinction—it is, nevertheless, a term which may be conveniently used to sum up the beliefs which motivated the performances known as Winter Ceremonials.

During these ceremonials dancers displayed the dances and songs they had obtained from the various supernatural spirits. As to do so required 'possession', either real or simulated, they took place at a time when communion with the spirits could be easily established. While spirits were never far from the Indian's world, they were believed to be closest, and therefore more readily contacted, during the cold months. Thus, winter was the 'Supernatural Season' or 'Time of Tabu' (a reference to ceremonial restrictions) when the major ceremonials were held. Also, it was a period when considerable time could be spent on religious pursuits, as the large gatherings essential for ceremonials

Left : An excellent sheet copper Tlingit 'Shakeyet' ceremonial headdress depicting a dog-fish with a smaller face on the forehead, inlaid with abalone.

were precluded during the summer months by the necessity of obtaining sufficient winter supplies.

Two main types of ceremonial can be readily distinguished: Spirit Singing and Dancing Societies. Spirit Singing entailed the display of an individual's powers which had been obtained through direct contact with a spirit during a dream or trance. Dancing Societies involved religious orders with ranked series of dancing positions, often parallel with the ranking within the households. The sequence of events leading to the acquisition of spirit powers by the ancestors was dramatized at these ceremonials. Positions in the Dancing Societies were strictly limited and could only be inherited by people with established ancestral claims to them.

In all probability, Spirit Singing was dominant in pre-contact times, as is suggested by its greater distribution in the surrounding areas and its continued use by shamans, who tended to be the more traditional and conservative members of the communities. The wealth brought by trade after the arrival of the Europeans increased the emphasis on status and rank in secular life, and, since they were closely linked, also altered the religious traditions. As a result, a similar rank structure was imposed during ceremonials and Spirit Singing began to be superseded by Dancing Societies with their hierarchies of privileged positions. Because the underlying principles of religious thought varied only slightly among the different groups, these rank elements spread rapidly— through inter-marriage, trade and warfare—until by the end of the nineteenth century the southern Salish were alone in retaining a complete Spirit Singing complex.

Dancing Societies were strongest among the northern Kwakiutl, also known as the Bella Bella or Heiltsuk, from whom they apparently spread to the neighbouring groups, many of whom used Kwakiutl names for their performers and sang songs in the Kwakiutl language. The Haida and Tsimshian attributed their dances directly to borrowings from the Bella Bella, and the Tlingit, by claiming a Tsimshian origin, were indirectly linked to the same source. Kwakiutl influence was also apparent among the Salish tribes on the north of Vancouver Island. Only the Nootkan Wolf Dance does not fit this pattern, but even this has many similarities with Kwakiutl ceremony, which makes some relationship between the two certain.

Ceremonials required carvings and paintings of totemic figures, which were quite distinct from those used on other occasions. A house was made sacred during the winter season by having the normal crests removed or covered up and replaced by the crests which belonged to the religious orders: the dancers frequently wore costumes which symbolized the characters of the spirits that were influencing them.

Salish carving, where dances were personal and status unimportant, was simple: often only a flat board with raised figures of the Otter or Mink, and simply carved statues of Welcoming Figures with outstretched arms. Although quite austere, these have a presence which is sometimes lacking in the art from other areas. The Kwakiutl, among whom status reached the point of obsession, went to the opposite extreme and by the late nineteenth century had developed gaudily painted carvings showing crest figures piled one above the other. Many of their earlier figures were extensively carved, and some were comparable with the simplicity of the Salish style. Later, incised lines were used to enclose painted areas and complex designs were painted directly on to flat surfaces—perhaps Kwakiutl carvers had difficulty keeping up with the increased demand for their work, caused by the upsurge in wealth goods, and therefore developed techniques by which apparently complicated carving could be completed more rapidly. Some of the Kwakiutl masks were multiple, carved with several heads or having a number of coverings which represented different aspects of the spirit's character and which could be exposed by pulling strings. They were always painted, and a number of them included copper bands fixed across the forehead or had copper discs as eyes, indicating the wealth of the family that owned them. They were usually attached to a cloak of cedar bark which covered the dancer's shoulders and when worn with a ceremonial costume this completely transformed the person into a representation of one of the mythical characters. As the masks got more elaborate they increased in size: a Hoxhok mask, representing a mythical bird which breaks men's skulls with its long beak, might be so large that it would have been impossible for its original owner to perform in it, unless he had attendants supporting its weight.

The art of other groups was affected by the increased splendour of the ceremonials in lesser degrees. Tlingit and Tsimshian art retained its delicacy and elegance, and their totem poles and masks show a subtle sense of colour. The Nootkans carved boldly and powerfully, although without the splendour of the Kwakiutl, and established themselves as mask makers and carvers for some of the southern tribes. Some of the

Above : Detail of a Tlingit box drum which would have been suspended from the rafters when in use. A killer-whale is painted on both sides. It formerly belonged to Chief Shakes but was given away by him in part payment for some slaves.

Left : The Coast Salish held only one masked dance in which this distinctive type of Xwé Xwé mask was used. The dance was associated with a super-natural being who had descended from the sky to spend his life at the bottom of a deep lake.

Far left : The Tlingit shaman some-times received his power through a vision in which the crane told him to climb on to its neck ; the bird then flew over great distances or dived beneath the sea. This old shaman's dance wand is carved with symbols of such a vision. The wand is in the shape of a crane which has a witch spirit on its beak and a reclining spirit shaman figure on its neck.

most impressive carving was made by the Haida, whose art had a sculptural quality which was unmatched elsewhere on the coast. It relied on interlocked figures which show a very highly developed sense of form and space and often used colour sparingly to emphasize important sculptured elements. Unfortunately, their woodworking tradition was affected very early and disastrously by population decline due to smallpox and other introduced diseases.

Since Salish Spirit Singing and Kwakiutl Dancing Societies represent the two opposites of northwest coast religious thought, comparison of their customs gives a picture of the religious practices of the entire area.

Among the Salish personal Guardian Spirits were obtained during the spirit-quest or, on relatively rare occasions, by a shaman 'breathing' spirit power into someone. In contrast with the Kwakiutl, who could only contact certain spirits if they had previously established rights to do so, any of the Salish could attempt to acquire power and there were no prestigious privileges associated with doing so. On the contrary, power involved strenuous obligations and was sometimes acquired against a person's will. Acquisition meant that a person was liable to become possessed at any time. Possession might be triggered, for example, by a sudden noise or a flash of light, especially in winter when the spirits were near by.

The ecstatic trance state which resulted from possession was called 'spirit-sickness', and this could only be cured by giving vent to emotion through Spirit Singing. Salish belief in this is so strong that even today failure to give expression to the possessive force causes actual physical illness. Spiritual power was not, however, attained through all supernatural encounters; a person would become symbolically dead, whereupon a shaman was called to him. He then would summon his Medicine Spirits if it was an ordinary illness to be cured. If the patient was to receive supernatural powers, the shaman would call his Dance Spirits.

If they were called, then the patient underwent an initiation procedure which has been described as 'like a torture', and which was intended to emphasize the strength required in handling powerful supernatural forces. It ensured the necessary endurance to withstand the demands of the dance that he would be required to perform at ceremonials. Shamanistic power assisted the inexperienced initiate during four days of ritual seclusion, at which a shaman's 'power-stick' and deer hoof rattles were always at hand. So, too, were the 'Baby-Minders', initiated dancers who woke him if he tried to sleep and kept him covered with a heavy blanket to make him sweat. They offered him food and water, and then snatched them away when he tried to eat or drink, and they beat incessant rhythms on deer skin drums held close to his head.

At the end of seclusion the initiate was 'reborn' and prepared to seek further visions in which he would learn the final form of his dance and song. Although these were individual, their expression required public acknowledgement. Thus, several related tribes would be invited to the Winter Ceremonials known as 'Dramatizations of Dreams'. If a dancer became possessed at some time of the year other than winter a minor ceremony was held immediately to enable him or her to perform to prevent permanent possession of the person by the spirit. This might take the form of a procession through the village, when the dancer would enter some of the more important houses—other dancers could be influenced by the proximity of the spirit if it was similar to their own and would also perform.

Right : This old Tsimshian mask is probably a portrait. The colour is particularly effective : red hand shapes on the cheeks draw attention to the mouth and the dancer's voice.

Right : This Chilkat Tlingit dance apron is woven from mountain goat wool and has been attached to a caribou-skin lining, which also forms the heavy fringe. Such aprons were worn round the waist on ceremonial occasions, but when not in use were carefully wrapped in cases made from bear intestines and stored in wooden boxes. The extreme care taken of them reflects their high value and the labour involved in their manufacture. One could take as much as a year to complete.

Far right : The painted border of a Haida chief's caribou-skin robe uses design shapes similar to those of Chilkat weaving, and the robe would have been worn at the same type of ceremonial occasion. The northwest coast habits of placing 'filler' designs in otherwise vacant spaces, eye symbols indicating joints, and the typical swelling line used to outline motifs, are well illustrated here.

During the Winter Ceremonials, when numerous different spirits were present, more than a hundred separate dancers might be inspired to perform in a single evening. The several groups from local tribes sat in tribal order around the sides of the Long-House, with each dancer joining the people who had been responsible for his initiation; for example, a man might sit with his wife's family rather than his own. Although this was considered to be a mark of respect, it was also essential since only the drummers accompanying that group knew, at least in theory, the rhythm of his secret song. Actually, many of the songs were quite formalized and had been performed several times each winter before the same groups, so everyone knew them even if this was not openly expressed. There was no ceremonial dress, except in the few costumed dances, but each dancer carried insignia peculiar to his own power and had an individual method of face-painting. If there was a mistake in the song or painting, it was believed that serious consequences, possibly death, would affect the entire group. There was, therefore, a tremendous social responsibility implied in these performances.

Men and women participated equally in the dances. There was an expectant atmosphere in the Salish Long-House as the dancers felt the presence of their spirits. One of them would become restless and begin to shake. As he lost conscious control of his actions he would call out to show his inner torment:

> 'Haiiii, hai, oh, o, o, o, o!
> Haiiii, hai, oh, o, o, o, o!
> Hai, ooooooh.
> Haiiii, hai, oh, o, o, o!'

The drummers from his initiating group crossed to where he sat and began to drum very softly, gently coaxing the spirit into complete possession. They were careful not to startle him since this could result in his power 'catching in his chest'. As he became more agitated the drumming grew louder. He gasped out a few words of his secret song in a faltering voice, and then gradually started to sing more confidently. Sometimes he became calmer for a few moments and the drumming subsided, but finally he leapt into the centre of the Long-House to dance.

The drummers accompanying the other groups picked up the rhythms as the dance progressed, until there were as many as two hundred people beating time. Two attendants circled the room with him, preventing him from crashing into the crowds of spectators lining the walls and guiding him clear of the central fires. They had difficulty at times in following some of the more unpredictable dance movements, when the dancer would hold a posture of rigid tension for several minutes and then suddenly rush forward. The movements of another dancer might be slow and undulating, representing possession by the Water Spirits, or perhaps mimicking the gestures of birds and animals by pausing cautiously or pawing the ground. Violent sobbing and wild frenzy were both very common.

Women's dances tended to be more sedate, while frenzied and exaggerated leapings were characteristic of the men's. Both were so intense, however, that a person was utterly exhausted by one circuit of the room, and had to be helped back to his seat where he collapsed in tears. It might take an hour or more for him to recover from the trance and return to his normal senses.

Dances were performed singly. Usually a performer completed a circuit of the Long-House before the drummers attempted to encourage the next participant, but, on occasions, a dancer might feel his spirit power so intensely that he would be compelled to start dancing before the previous person had finished. This caused a certain amount of confusion, since the drummers followed two different sets of rhythms,

while the presence of an additional possessive spirit heightened the spiritual atmosphere in the house. In fact, the tension might begin to affect other people who would also begin to feel their spirits influencing them more strongly. Generally, it was the responsibility of the older and more experienced dancers in the host tribe to restore order by assisting the younger dancers and new initiates to control their emotions, and by regulating the intensity of the drumming.

An Indian dancer gave this description of the experience of possession:

'When you sing your breath starts shaking. After a while it goes into you. You try to sing, your jaws start to shake, then you sing it out, you get over it. When I dance I don't act, just follow your power, just follow the way of your power.' (Wolfgang Jilek *Salish Indian Mental Health and Culture Change* p. 27.)

Since the Salish did not have the closely knit kin groups of the northern tribes, their ceremonials were vital in maintaining inter-group contacts. Even more important, though, was the psychological effect they had on the participants. Younger dancers established a place for themselves in society, and gained confidence through public recognition of their identity. With the help of the group, pride in one's achievements could be demonstrated, respect extended to those of others, and any tensions created by emotional problems could be dispelled. Help was always willingly given, and in fact the spirits were said to be closer to a person during periods of personal stress. Today Spirit Singing among the Salish—now referred to as Indian Dancing—remains as a very effective method of tackling personal difficulties, and is frequently successful where modern medical practices have failed, particularly in the treatment of psychosomatic disorders.

The most northerly Salish tribes had little contact with their southern neighbours—their dialects were so different that they could not even understand each other—and many aspects of their ceremonies were quite different. Parts of them involved displays of showmanship and trickery (a distinctive Kwakiutl trait), and had masked figures similar to those of the Kwakiutl. Although spirit possession was still a requirement it may have been simulated, or it was derived from ancestral powers which had been handed down as privileges, thus combining the basic principles of Spirit Singing with hereditary prestige.

In contrast to the Salish Spirit Singing, Kwakiutl ceremonials were highly formalized with considerable emphasis on prestige, as in all their social activities. During Tsetseka, the Supernatural Season, their entire social order was considerably changed, and a system based on a ranked order of spirits and Dancing Societies was adopted. People could only be addressed by ceremonial names, with severe penalties for any infringements; seating at festivities followed dancing positions instead of families and clans; words associated with particular spirits were tabu and the circumlocution 'salmonberries' used in their stead; and important houses had the crests removed and replaced by Society crests. All normal activities came to an abrupt stop at the sound of the whistling which announced the arrival of the spirits.

There were three mutually exclusive Kwakiutl Dancing Societies, sometimes known as Secret Societies, each of which had a number of fixed dancing positions ranked in order of importance. They differed mainly in the types of spirits with which each was associated. The Shamans' Society, whose membership was not restricted to shamans, was connected with an array of fearsome and violent supernatural characters. Of these a cannibal figure was the most prestigious, and a position as a cannibal-dancer, or Hamatsa, could only be occupied by a member of a chiefly lineage.

In the Dluwulaxa Society, or Those-Who-Descend-from-the-Heavens, the spirits involved were those of the skies. An initiate supposedly went

Masks representing natural elements were used in the Dluwulaxa and crest dances. Shown here is a Kwakiutl sun mask with an eagle's face carved in its centre. The style is very similar to masks made by the Bella Coola, and may illustrate the borrowing of dance concepts through intermarriage. It is certain that the Bella Coola had a strong influence on the Kwakiutl.

to these upper regions to receive a dance position from them, becoming a dancer on the occasion of his descent to earth. The third Society, Nutlam, is usually referred to in English as the Dog-Eaters since this was a characteristic of their mythical ancestors, the Wolves.

All the Societies had visually startling theatrical performances which featured masked dancers. Kwakiutl Winter Ceremonials were held on the occasion of a new member's initiation, with the established members officiating and acting in a supportive role; they would perform their own dances but the initiate was the principal performer. He disappeared and theoretically retraced his ancestor's steps to the supernatural world, where the original gift of songs and dances was repeated. On his return in a possessed state he was restored to his senses by esoteric purification rites from which non-initiates were barred. The public parts of these Winter Ceremonials were marked by complex magical tricks which

Above : Abalone shell ornaments were attached to the plaited cedar bark headring of a Kwakiutl Hamatsa dancer. These were worn during the Tsetseka, or red cedar bark, dance season and the headring was dyed red by being steeped in alder bark juice. Initiates could be identified by peculiarities of the plaiting and by their ornaments.
Right : The Speaker's Staff, or Chief's Talking Stick, was tapped on the floor to gain attention before important announcements were made. This Kwakiutl staff is carved with a variety of figures, some of which are holding coppers. Similar staffs were used by the Sparrow Society when calling guests to the dance house, by certain dancers to indicate their dancing positions, and by shamans.

were intended to convince the audience that the performance was genuine.

The description which follows is of the initiation of a chief's son as a Hamatsa dancer in the Shamans' Society. This was the most elaborate ceremony, but a similar procedure was followed for other Shamans' positions and for initiations into the Dluwulaxa and Nutlam—details, of course, varied according to the natures of the different spirits.

Since Society positions were limited, a vacancy had to arise before a new member could be initiated. This sometimes happened through a member's death but was more commonly the result of an older person's 'retirement'. The intention to retire was announced by the bride's father during her marriage ceremony, when he promised to relinquish his privilege of Society membership and pass it over to one of her children. He would then join the ranks of the 'old men', former members who retained the right to attend Society meetings but who were not active dancers. If this was the Hamatsa privilege, then the boy had to be initiated into one or more of the lower dance orders before the promise could be fulfilled. These were very simple and required four days of ritual seclusion and purification. By becoming a minor dancer when he was about twelve years old a person was ready to become a Hamatsa in his late teens or early twenties.

A year or so before the Hamatsa initiation the bride's father, his son-in-law and members of the Sparrow Society (former dancers who functioned as shamans and ensured that the details of ritual procedure were correct) held several meetings to discuss the amount of the marriage gift repayment, and made preliminary arrangements for inviting neighbouring tribes. The acceptance of an invitation and the arrival of the guests followed the same procedure as that for a potlatch, which was usually given at the same time.

A man holding the right to make the important announcements on the father-in-law's behalf, called the Speaker, carried a ceremonial staff carved with crest figures before the guests into the centre of the Big-House. This represented the value of the property to be given away, and by touching it the initiate formally indicated his acceptance of the amount. Everyone now spent four days in ritual purification.

Whistles, the voices of the spirits, could be heard when the people reassembled. At first the sound came from the woods behind the village, but it gradually drew closer until, suddenly, there was a violent hammering on the roof boards and whistles were blowing all around the house. The initiate called the Cannibal cry—'Hap! Hap! Hap!'—and used the confusion caused by the appearance of the spirits as an opportunity to slip unnoticed through a secret exit. Almost immediately his cry was heard again, this time from the distant woods (where another Society member had hidden himself) as the spirits rapidly transported him away from the village. He was said to have been taken to the house of Baxbakualanuxsiwae, the Cannibal-at-the-North-End-of-the-World, where he would remain for up to four months. In reality, he remained close to the village and received instructions in the Society's rites and formalities.

The house was made sacred while the initiate was absent. A cedar bark ring, the symbol of supernatural power, was hung over the doorway, and a rope was stretched from the gable to the water's edge to prevent anyone passing in front. Other activities were carried on secretly and included making new masks, ceremonially preparing the house interior, which consisted mainly of installing devices used in the performance of magic and replacing the crests, and composing new words for the spirit songs.

Several boxes of property, one of which contained the Hamatsa's dance paraphernalia, were given to the initiate's father by his father-in-law. These were used to build a symbolic canoe on the beach, which was later 'sunk' by breaking the boxes open and distributing the wealth. Meanwhile, numerous incidental dances and other social activities took place before the Hamatsa would reappear.

A ceremony designed to bring him back was given by the Seal Society (the dancers who impersonated spirits). With the exception of the Hamatsas, who were also Seals but had the door of the Big-House barred against them on this occasion, they sang their new spirit songs. These were individual and, since they all sang at once, the chants quickly became confused, indicating that many equally powerful spirit influences were present. In the early evening the Ghost-Dancers mimicked a journey to the Land of the Dead.

Since the dead lived beneath the real world, ghostly voices were heard coming from the centre of the fire (the connection between the upper and lower regions). Hollow kelp stems buried under the earth floor connected the fireplace with the secret room at the rear of the house, and were used as speaking tubes to achieve this effect. The Ghosts' activities aroused the Hamatsas, who 'had been all around the world looking for corpses', and they began to beat on the outside of the house. Finding the door barred, they burst their way through the walls calling 'Hap! Hap! Hap!' An answering shout came from the roof, and the initiate, who was now possessed by Baxbakualanuxsiwae's desires for human flesh, pushed aside a plank and jumped down, whereupon the Seals tried to catch him, causing him to flee from them through the rear exit.

It was essential that he was caught and 'tamed', that is restored to his senses. The Seals therefore went out to search at the Place-of-Super-natural-Power (a lake or river used for ritual bathing). Although they found and surrounded him, he escaped from them by disappearing, reappearing instantly on the other side of the village—an impersonator had really been surrounded, and had vanished by changing his hemlock clothing for the cedar bark costume of the Society while screened by them from the onlookers at the village.

After several unsuccessful attempts it was obvious that he could not be caught this way, so it was decided to try trickery. One of the Seals danced naked in front of the group. His nudity appealed to the Hamatsa who had a voracious appetite for human flesh and he was immediately attacked by the initiate who bit a large piece out of his arm. With his desire for flesh partially satisfied, he allowed himself to be captured and led to the house, but he refused to enter. Struggling free, he climbed to the roof and pulled the ladders up after him to prevent pursuit. The Hamatsa's female attendant, the Kinqalalala, now tried to entice him into the house by dancing backwards through the door and singing her secret song. She was nude and may have carried a corpse, or a corpse effigy, in her arms, representing the slave in the origin-myth who lured men into Baxbakualanuxsiwae's house, and then killed them for her master.

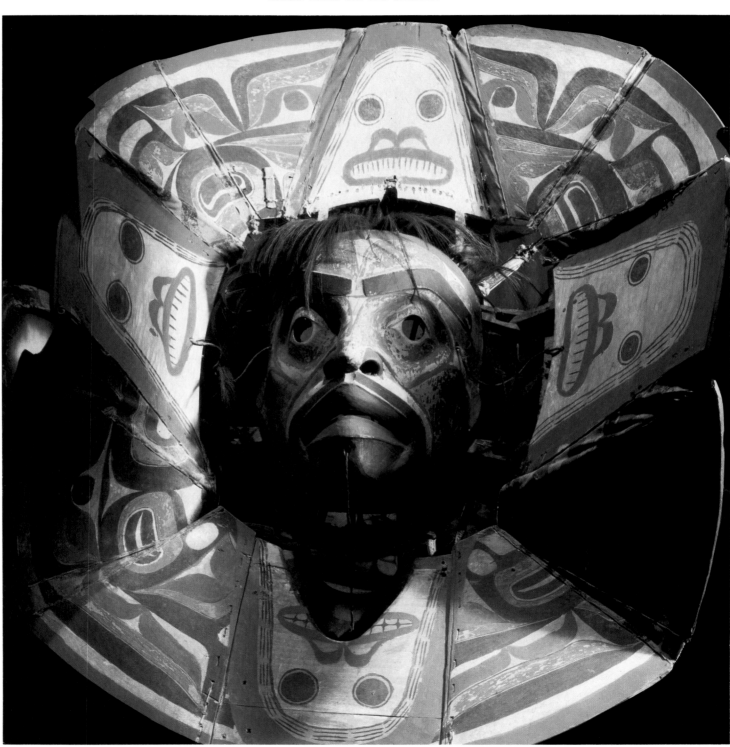

Eventually the initiate responded, but on entering he bit the arm of a person standing near the door and then fled back to the roof. On the Kinqalalala's fourth attempt he became subdued enough to be taken to a secret room at the rear of the house where he was ceremonially tied to the Cannibal Pole. This provided a link with the natural world and prevented the spirits reclaiming him. The whole episode had been carefully prearranged because being bitten was a right, owned by few people, who rubbed ash into the wounds to leave a scar to display their privilege.

The Hamatsa would now shake the Cannibal Pole furiously if he became excited, and could only be quieted when he was led from the secret room, securely tethered to a stout rope held by two strong men, to perform his Cannibal Song:

'Ham ham amai, ham ham amai, hamai, hamaima mamai, hamai hamamai.

   Ham hamam ham am ham amamai hamei hamamai.

   Ham ham amai. Utter the Hamatsa cry, utter the Hamatsa cry, the cry of the great spirit who dwells at the north end of the world.

   Ham ham amai. Utter Baxbakualanuxsiwae's cry, Baxbakualanux-siwae's cry, the cry of the great spirit who dwells at the north end of the world.

   Ham ham amai. Utter the Hoxhok cry, the Hoxhok cry, the cry of the great spirit who dwells at the north end of the world.

   Ham ham amai. Utter the Raven cry, the Raven cry, the cry of the great spirit who dwells at the north end of the world.' (Boas *Social Organization* p. 458.)

While singing he danced in a crouched position, indicating that he was possessed. Every so often he would try to bite members of the audience, and was only prevented from doing so by his attendants' pulling on the rope. As the song pacified him he began to dance upright, until finally he was calmed and could be taken back to his room.

These periods of frenzied behaviour were often provoked by a breach of one of the tabus in force, such as using a secular name instead of a

Left : The Haida had an incomplete Hamatsa dance series, believed to have been obtained from the Kwakiutl, in which masks were used to display privileges. This Haida mosquito mask opens to reveal a human face surrounded by paintings of the dog-fish. Although insects were comic characters in some Kwakiutl Hamatsa dances, this mask was probably associated with a clan origin myth.

Above : The Kwakiutl Hamatsa hungers for human flesh and, to indicate his predilection, his regalia were often decorated with carved wooden skulls such as those in the centre and right. That on the left is of a type carried on a board by the Hamatsa's female attendant, the Kinqalalala, during her dance to placate him and entice him into the house.

religious one, or saying 'dead' instead of using the circumlocution 'salmonberries'. These tabus tended to reinforce the fact that the ceremonial was being held at a sacred time of the year; their breach 'offended' the spirits possessing the initiated. Frenzy was also contagious, and during the initiate's performance it was quite common for all the older Hamatsas to become excited and attempt to bite people.

One of the ways that spirit possession manifested was in behaviour which was considered inhuman, and in acts which no person would do of his own volition. Eating human flesh was utterly repugnant but at the height of the Hamatsa's ecstasy he ate a human corpse. The Kwakiutl had a very pronounced fear of the dead, and the abhorrence caused to people in their normal senses by this act was a testimony to the Hamatsa's possession.

The Hamatsa's attitude is vividly conveyed in this song:

> 'Now I am going to eat.
> My face is ghastly pale.
> I shall eat what is given to me by Cannibal-
>   at-the-North-End-of-the-World.'
>   (Boas *Social Organization* p. 459.)

There is some doubt as to whether actual corpses were used. The Kwakiutl were masters of the magic trick and it is quite feasible that the 'corpses' were animal skin dummies with realistically carved wooden heads like the portrait heads which were convincingly used during the 'decapitation' of some dancers. By the half-light of the fire they could easily have passed for the real thing.

All the songs, dances, biting of people and cannibalism had, then, been directed toward pacifying the Hamatsa, who was believed to be the actual incarnation of the Cannibal spirit. He was finally tamed by symbolically placing the Winter Ceremonial secrets in pieces of white cedar bark and burning them. The potlatch following this action concluded the public parts of the ceremonial. Due to the long period of possession, however, the initiate was still under the spirits' influence. He was believed to be bereft of all human qualities, and had to be taught how to walk and speak. Lengthy purification rites then had to be held, at which the paraphernalia was burnt and the smoke used as a purifying agent. The rites were held in secret, with the door to the house securely closed and chinks in the wall boards covered. The initiate was also subject to tabu restrictions for up to four years: for the first few months he ate only warm food as the spirits ate cold food and he had to readjust; he refrained from sexual relationships for a year; and he was forbidden to gamble or work. Usually he displayed the masks he had been given for four successive winters before he became a fully fledged member of the Shamans' Society.

Below the Hamatsa were other dance positions in the Shamans' Society: the Hamshamtses, a female equivalent of the Hamatsa who was slightly more sedate since she only bit people and did not eat corpses; Nontsistalal, or Fire-Thrower, who had the annoying habit of throwing live coals around in the houses he visited—he wore a small piece of damp deer skin over the palm of his hand which enabled him to handle fire; and Nulmal, the Fool-Dancer, who, with the help of Grizzly-Bear-Dancer, threw stones at people or hit them with sticks and lances if they broke tabu restrictions.

The Dluwulaxa Society operated on the same principles as the Shamans', differing in that their initiates disappeared to the sky from which they were called down by several days of singing. Their spirit impersonations lacked the violent characteristics of the Shamans' dancers, and only the War Spirit, who spent four days breaking objects and striking things with his fists, caused any damage. All the rest danced quietly and made extensive use of articulated masks such as the Sun

Below : Nulmal hated anything that was clean and orderly. He was violent and filthy, wore old clothing, and had matted, greasy hair. His mask has a prominent nose, reflecting his concern with mucus, and the features are carved to look repulsive.
Right : A northern Kwakiutl mask, similar to others which represent the sun. It has a nose shape which curves down and touches the face in the characteristic symbol of a hawk's beak.
Right, below : Tsimshian carving manages to convey a uniquely individual expression. The genial, round face on this moon mask suggests a non-aggressive character. The smoothly finished surface, typical of Tsimshian work, shows the artist's good knowledge of facial structure.

mask. In its closed position this represented the sun, but, at an appropriate moment in the dance, the dancer turned away from the audience, turning back with the outer cover opened (by use of strings) to reveal an inner face depicting the human character of the spirit. Other articulated masks were used to demonstrate changes in character by revealing alternately sombre and angry faces, or had interchangeable parts, such as several mouthpieces, which were deftly swapped while passing the hands in front of the face.

The Dluwulaxa and Shamans' Societies were approximately equal in the status that membership gave to their dancers: the War-Spirit Dancer, the highest Dluwulaxa position, had almost equivalent rank to the Hamatsa; Healing-Dancer, second position in the Dluwulaxa, enjoyed rank equal to the second Shamans' dancer, Fire-Thrower. Some dances in the Dluwulaxa series, however, required greater expenditure since they were given together with the most important potlatches. Nutlam was of lesser importance to the Kwakiutl and without any ranked dance positions, but it enjoyed a wider distribution than the others among the different language groups.

It was possible to receive a dance privilege without being initiated by assuming that of an opponent defeated in war, since he had already

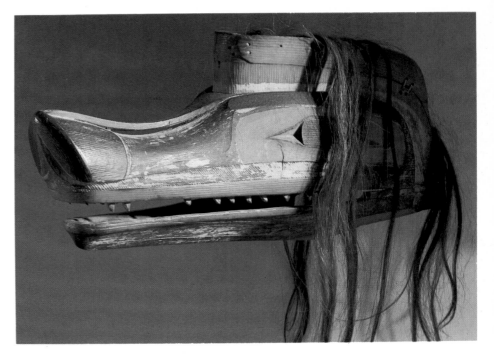

Below : Tlingit frontlet depicting a beaver with a frog between his paws. This was attached to a stick frame with ermine skins, swan's down and sea-lion bristles, and was worn over the dancer's forehead.
Right : This old wolf mask is probably Nootkan since it is made by steaming and bending the wood rather than carving. It was not worn during the Wolf Dance, but was used as a display privilege.
Far right : When making a portrait mask the northwest coast artist did not have to attempt a realistic interpretation. Since they were the same as those used in facial painting, the painted designs were symbols of the mask owners. A flat upper lip and broad nose indicate that this mask is Haida.

undergone initiation. A Tlingit, for example, could defeat a Kwakiutl Hamatsa and use the dance in his own Shamans' Society. There was sufficient contact between the groups and enough similarity in their customs for him to have a fairly accurate idea of the rituals associated with the position; all he required was the right to ownership of the privilege to allow him to display the dance. Kwakiutl influence may have spread to other groups in this manner and it would also explain why many of them had an incomplete dance series, as they may have been unaware of the entire procedure. In fact, Tlingit, Tsimshian and Haida all used derivatives of Kwakiutl names for their Societies.

Among the Tlingit there was a tendency to consider the dances as personal privileges which could be used as display crests during potlatches, and consequently they did not have so much importance as communal affairs. They even referred to the later performances as 'just a show', although they regarded the ancestral contacts as genuine.

In common with nearly all the other coastal peoples, the Tlingit had a Dog-Eaters' Society whose rituals included tearing apart and devouring a live dog. As this was said to be a characteristic of wolves, it showed the initiate's inspiration by Wolf Spirits. The function it served was the same as Hamatsa cannibalism since dog flesh was believed to be poisonous to a person in his normal state. Indeed, so firmly ingrained was this belief that an Indian would normally sooner have suffered starvation than eat his dogs.

The Tlingit might perform large ceremonials outside the Big-House. The dancers used certain movements of the head and shoulders which were descriptive of the spirits being represented. Animal movements were very common, and the dancer stopped every few steps to pause and turn his head, showing, perhaps, the Wolf being pursued. The movements of the feet did not vary during the course of the dance and the body was held tense, giving an effect of jerky motion but conveying an impression of controlled power.

They used fewer full masks than most of the other groups. Instead, in common with the Tsimshian, they wore a type of headdress with long streamers of ermine which was known as a forehead mask or frontlet from the way in which it was worn. These were quite small and delicately carved, and were extensively inlaid with small pieces of abalone shell. Among their dancers, the Raven painted his face with an abstract symbol of Raven's beak and wore coiled rings of cedar bark on his head; the Bear Dancer's hands were made to represent paws;

and the Killer-Whale Dancer wore a mask with a tall dorsal fin on top of his head, while his movements imitated the whale diving.

Their Society crests were regarded as recent introductions from the Tsimshian, or had been purchased as property from the Alaskan Kaigani-Haida, who had a very great number of dances in both the Shamans' and Dog-Eaters' Societies. Haida dances of the Alaskan group and of the main tribes on the Queen Charlotte Islands differed from those of the Kwakiutl only in that the ranked positions were less sharply differentiated, and that their chiefs were often members of two societies. An unusual aspect of the Haida was their restrained use of very abstract facial painting in depicting their spirits, a line or a few dots expressing the complete character. Their old masks are frequently surmounted with hair or a 'crown' of sea-lion bristles.

The closest group to the Kwakiutl was the southern coast Tsimshian, and the influence of the Kwakiutl ranked dances on them is quite evident. Most of their dances were borrowed from their Kwakiutl-speaking neighbours, the Bella Bella, but they retained a strong interest in personal Guardian Spirits. For example, the Cannibal Dancer became the guardian of certain chiefly lineages but did not feature in any Society.

The southern coast Tsimshian had two Dancing Societies—the Dog-Eaters and the Mitla, or Dancers. The dances of the latter derived from the myth of a young man who repeatedly visited the sky until one day he failed to return to earth. The tale is very similar to the Kwakiutl myth which tells of Those-Who-Descend-from-the-Heavens, and even the word *Mitla* is derived from a Kwakiutl word *Meitla*.

Positions in the Tsimshian Societies were not hereditary but a person joined the group of his sponsor. Families went to considerable lengths to gain the advantages of having members in both Societies because they could then establish some connection with all the important families in the tribe. However, not everybody belonged to a Society and a personal spirit helper was considered equally beneficial. It was mandatory for every child to undergo a 'power-ceremony' in which he received some spirit assistance. A second ceremony entitled him to a 'power-name' and prepared him for Society membership. The ceremonies were conducted by chiefs who threw their power into a child concealed beneath a blanket in a corner of the room, and an answering whistle indicated that it had been received. Many of the children were babies when this was done, so their mothers accompanied them and blew the whistles.

Substitution was sometimes employed in the Society initiations too; a relative, or even a slave, played the initiate's role, particularly if there was danger involved and the initiate was the chief's daughter. They also sang the songs if the child was too young to remember all the words, and performed the difficult dances for him. The main difference between the power ceremony and an initiation was that the latter involved disappearance. A trick was often used to make the person reappear: he returned riding on the back of a crest, probably a canoe with a structure representing the crest animal built over it, or he might walk on the water by weighting a raft with heavy stones so that it floated just below the surface. These ceremonies were repeated to obtain higher status, and the more important people usually went through them four times.

Another group in close contact with the Kwakiutl were the Bella Coola. Belonging to the Coast Salish language group, but living in the middle of Kwakiutl territory, they had a culture, in every respect, almost identical with that of the Bella Bella, their Kwakiutl neighbours. Both had a War Spirit—Toxwid to the Bella Bella and Self-Destroying-Spirit to the Bella Coola—which was indestructible, regardless of the wounds it received. In order to show this the spirit would invite people to kill it and then, through the use of elaborate stage properties, miraculously resurrect itself. Toxwid was a female spirit, therefore impersonated by a young woman. Her well-documented tricks are in most ways similar to those of her Bella Coola counterpart.

Above and right : In order to show various attributes of the same name during Tsimshian dance performances, masks often had articulated features. The eyes of this mask have three positions : open, closed and copper-covered ; the jaw moves to reveal either a set of teeth or a copper band. It was not unusual for these portrait masks to be made in sets, showing different stages in a person's life. A woman's masks might show her, for example, as a young unmarried girl, in middle age, as a wealthy old lady, and shortly after death—indicated by half-closed or inverted eyes.

In one of Toxwid's tricks she climbed into a box which was placed on the fire and burnt, and as the flames consumed it her voice could be heard calling from them. Her bones were then collected from the ashes and placed under a blanket, and she came back to life. To accomplish this a box with a false bottom was placed over a pit in which a skeleton had previously been hidden. Toxwid substituted this and then covered the pit opening with a cedar bark mat. The pit had a speaking tube connecting it with the fireplace, and an underground passage led to a second pit above which the bones were placed.

Her most accomplished feat involved her supernatural spirit, the Sisiutl. While she was dancing, Sisiutl, a double-headed serpent, rose

up out of the floor in front of her. She took hold of it by the horns and it began to pull her under. Although several men tried to stop it by holding her around the waist and straining against Sisiutl's power, they were unable to do so. Finally she was completely underground but one of the men refused to let go. He was pulled down as far as his elbows, and then dragged around the dance floor. His arms ploughed up mounds of earth, as the Sisiutl tried to shake him off.

Extensive preparations had been made to stage this when the house was closed for ritual cleansing. A pit had been dug, in which a man with a Sisiutl carving was concealed and into which Toxwid vanished. The crowd who had tried to rescue her gathered around when this happened so that she had sufficient time to place a mat over the pit opening, thus concealing it from the audience. Running in a zigzag around the house was a shallow trench, in which a cedar bark rope had been laid and covered with loose earth. The man who was dragged through the house actually pulled himself along this rope.

Toxwid could also perform less elaborate tricks such as making an object rattle which remained mute for others, however hard they tried. She could send objects flying through the air and call them back to her. Both of these were simply managed, the first with pebbles concealed in her ceremonial wristband, and the second by lines attached to the roof.

The entertaining nature of these performances was not without a serious purpose since they relieved the more violent aspects shown in other dances. Some dancers played a humorous role and acted as clowns. They mimicked the actions of the serious performances and parodied the more pretentious chiefs. They would also look into the secret room and give jocular accounts of the initiate's condition, constantly explaining the 'real truth' to the audience.

In contrast to the Bella Coola, the Nootkan tribes, on the far coast of Vancouver Island, were distant from Kwakiutl influence. Consequently, their ceremonial did not feature awe-inspiring and monstrous spirits. They had only one major ceremony, known as Loqwana, which translates as 'Shamans' but which is actually based on a wolf myth similar to the Dog-Eaters', and is generally referred to as the Wolf Dance. The same ceremony is found among the southern Kwakiutl at Quatsino Sound.

In the Nootkan origin-myth, an ancestor visited the House of the Wolves where he was taught songs and dances. Returning home he discovered that he had been away for four years, although he thought it was only four days, and that he was still possessed by the Wolf Spirits. The Wolf Dance substituted a kidnapping for the original visit, but the remainder was a dramatization of his rescue from the Wolf Spirits' influence.

The ceremonial began with the kidnapping of a group of young children to be initiated by men wearing conventionalized Wolf disguises—although Wolf masks were very common among the Nootka, they were not used in this ceremonial but were kept as symbols of personal privilege. Sometimes the kidnapping was symbolized by finding the initiates' clothing, torn to shreds, lying on the beach. In either case, tabu restrictions immediately came into force and preparations were made for the rescue.

The Nootkans introduced a great deal of levity into their Wolf Dance, probably because the initiates were young children, and would have been terrified by the procedures followed by other groups. For example, the parents of the kidnapped children were accused of carelessness—'You should watch your children more carefully, then the Wolves couldn't steal them'—and were thrown into the sea as a punishment. There was also considerable energy expended in goading people into breaking tabus, and a transgressor was punished by having all his or her clothes ripped off. During the ceremony eating alone was prohibited so anyone who felt hungry had to turn the occasion into a feast

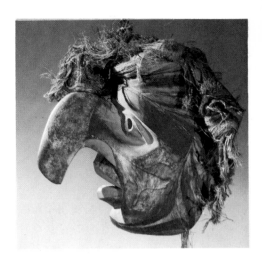

*Left : Said to represent an ancestor
who assumed the form of an eagle, the
projection on this Bella Coola mask
has a closer resemblance to the nose
shape of a type of Kwakiutl Nulmal
than it does to an eagle's beak.*
*Below : This club refers to the capture
of a Nootkan novice, when the Wolves
were said to carry off uninitiated
people in their teeth. It may have been
used as a display object to represent the
powers its owner received during his
captivity.*

and invite others. This turned the period into a constant round of
socializing which prevented anyone avoiding his obligation to participate
in the children's initiation.

Search parties were organized by a group of people who went through
the village looking for the children in the early hours of the morning,
tipping people out of bed and throwing icy water over them, but the
searches proved fruitless and it was decided to attract the Wolves by
ceremonial drumming. This was conducted by a drum leader who
climbed to the roof of the Big-House, where he was to watch for supernatural signs and indicate to the drummers in the house when it was
necessary to make a concerted effort. In accordance with Nootkan
humour, the drumming developed into a farce with the leader claiming
he was unable to hear the drums, even though there may have been a
hundred or more of them beating, and the drummers accusing him of
being useless.

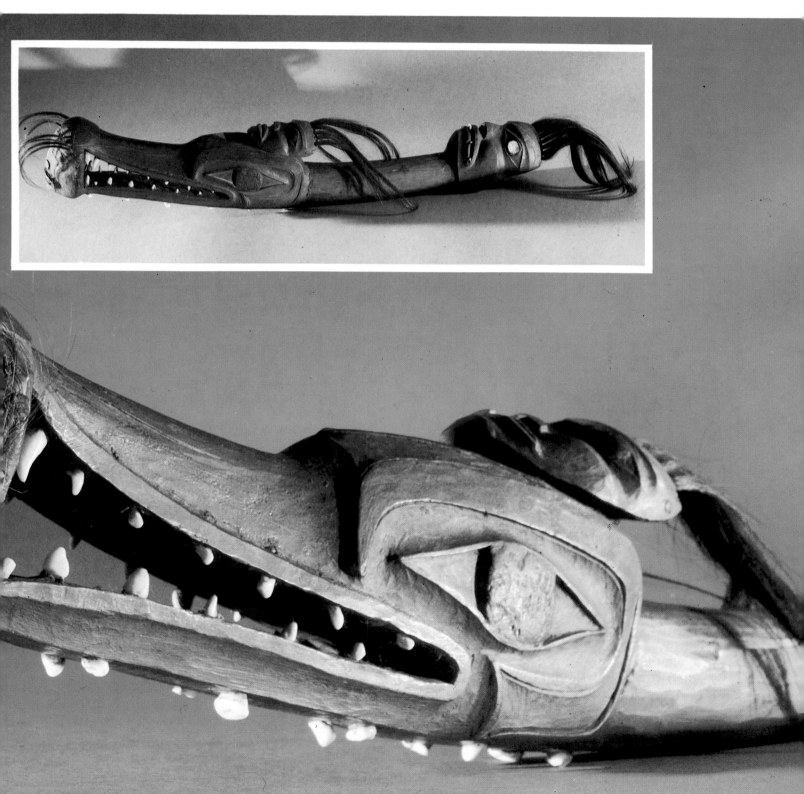

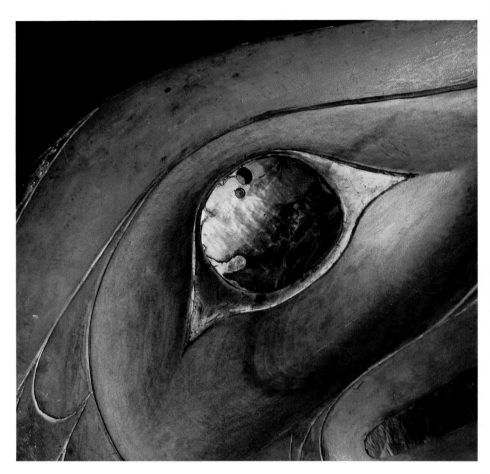

Eventually, however, the drumming proved successful and the sound of whistling Wolves could be heard outside the house. At a signal from their leader the drummers stopped, and the initiates could be heard singing their secret songs or calling out that they were captives of the Wolves, who then took them away again.

In order to facilitate their rescue, a group of 'Wolf experts' prepared their traps—giant halibut hooks, or flimsy constructions of twigs and netting—and the next morning a flotilla of canoes and rafts set out across the bay. When they were about half way across, the Wolves appeared on the opposite shore, causing consternation among the boats. Some people feigned terror and turned back, 'accidentally' knocking against the 'experts' and tipping them into the water if they could. Meanwhile the Wolves disappeared.

When the boats finally beached, the Wolves reappeared further along the shore and the experts rushed off to attack them, tripping each other over and becoming hopelessly entangled in the lines of their wolf traps in the process. Their actions were said to have a serious purpose, to distract the Wolves' attention so that they left their captives unguarded. Four times the Wolves appeared and retreated before the attacks, each time moving away from the initiates. Seizing their opportunity, the people helped them into the boats and pushed out to sea, leaving the experts behind to escape the enraged maulings of the Wolves as best they could. (They would later strut proudly through the village telling everyone about how they had almost killed a Wolf.)

Upon the children's return to the village, the songs and dances which the Wolves had given them were demonstrated. Since these were hereditary rights, a person with several to claim would be kidnapped on a number of occasions. Spirit contamination was removed by ritual purification which involved burning the ceremonial costumes the children had worn, and a period of seclusion. A potlatch finalized the festivities.

The Winter Ceremonials were the major social event on the northwest coast. For five months of each year the stores of preserved food made it possible for people to spend their time in feasting and dancing, and in celebrating their spirits. Since the Indian was so close to nature, he had a high regard for its powerful forces and a genuine humility in the face of them. He transferred the forces to the 'other world', a place peopled with numerous spirits who were both fearsome and very human, and out of this concept developed a religion demanding mutual co-operation.

A very obvious and sincere belief that a spirit personally assisted each individual was expressed during Salish Spirit Singing, and the society actively endorsed this fact. Although the Dancing Society members were aware of the simulation involved in their representations, their faith was at least as strong as that of the Salish; the events from the generations of ancestors had a 'hidden reality' which could only be understood by thorough knowledge (initiation) of the esoteric mysteries of the Society.

As a reflection of the spirit of the northwest coast, the Winter Ceremonial drew together all aspects of an individual's life and reaffirmed his beliefs, presenting them in a dramatic and vivid manner. For the Indian, steeped in centuries of tradition, this was not merely a performance. The dance told of the glories belonging to the past and made promises for the future; it gave importance and recognition when it was needed; and it allowed freedom of expression. The power of the drummers, the drama of the masks, and the seemingly impossible supernatural events which took place, would have made an outsider wonder whether it had been an illusion. The strength and sophistication of the events were such that those who watched were convinced of the reality of the dance.

Acknowledgments

Werner Forman and the publishers would like to acknowledge the help of the following museums and private collections in permitting the photography shown on the pages listed:
The Trustees of the British Museum, London, England: 4, 18 top, 33, 53, 54, 67, 87, 111, 122–123. Centennial Museum, Vancouver, British Columbia, Canada: 9 top, 11 bottom, 101 top. Ex-collection James Cooper, Watersfield, England: 67, 95. Denver Art Museum, Colorado, USA: 29, 118 top. Field Museum of Natural History, Chicago, USA: endpapers, 1, 13 top, 14, 24, 31 top, 34, 37 bottom, 46 top, 56, 59, 70 left, 80, 84, 104, 108–109. Mr John H. Haubert: 119. Joslyn Art Museum, Omaha, Nebraska, USA: 18 bottom. McCord Museum, Montreal, Canada: 35. Museum of Anthropology, University of British Columbia, Vancouver, Canada: 11 top, 13 bottom, 28, 41, 48, 61 top, 64, 73, 96, 99, 113. Museum of the American Indian, Heye Foundation, USA: 93, 106–107. National Museum of Man, Ottawa, Ontario, Canada: 15, 31 bottom, 36 top, 37 top, 45, 50, 60, 63, 79, 82, 88, 101 bottom, 105, 114, 118 bottom. Portland Art Museum, Oregon, USA: 34 left and right, 86, 102, 105 top right. Provincial Museum, Victoria, British Columbia, Canada: 12, 16, 30, 32, 42, 43, 46 bottom, 47, 58, 61 bottom, 62, 66 top, 72 bottom, 76–77, 78, 81, 97, 98, 112, 115, 117, 118, 120, 121, 122 top, 124. Mr and Mrs John A. Putnam: 72–73. Private collection: 17, 66 bottom. Private collection, Ketchikan, Alaska, USA: 85. Royal Ontario Museum, Toronto, Canada: 55, 74, 75, 83, 100, 116. University Museum, Philadelphia, Pennsylvania, USA: 44. University Museum, Seattle, Washington, USA: 27.

Werner Forman would also like to thank the following for their assistance:
Dennis Alsford, Dave Bruckner, Madeline Bronsdon, Helen Chandra, Ralph Coe, Richard Daily, Dr Fuchs, Trisha Gessler, Lenore Johnstone, Jonathan King, Sherie Koutz, Catherine Lampert, Lynn Maranda, Tom Martin, Peter L. Mcnair, Margaret Patterson, Inge Ruus, Dr Stiles, Ron Webber.

Bibliography

Beaglehole, J. C. (ed.) *The Journals of Captain James Cook* Vol. III, parts 1 and 2, Cambridge University Press, Cambridge 1967

Boas, Franz *Ethnology of the Kwakiutl* 35th Annual Report of the Bureau of American Ethnology, Smithsonian Institution, 1913–14, Government Printing Office, Washington 1921
Primitive Art Dover Publications, New York 1955 (repr.)
The Social Organisation and Secret Societies of the Kwakiutl Indians, Annual Report for 1895 of the U.S. National Museum, Smithsonian Institution, Washington 1897

Inverarity, Robert Bruce *Art of the Northwest Coast Indians* University of California Press, Berkeley and London 1973 (5th ed.)

Jacobsen, Johan Adrian *Alaskan Voyage 1881–83* (trans. Erna Gunther) University of Chicago Press, Chicago and London 1977

Jewitt, John R. *Narrative of the Adventures and Suffering of John R. Jewitt* Edinburgh 1824

Jilek, Wolfgang G. *Salish Indian Mental Health and Culture Change* Holt, Rinehart and Winston, Toronto, Ontario 1974

Powell, Jay and Jensen, Vickie *Quileute: an Introduction to the Indians of La Push* University of Washington Press, Seattle and London 1976

Index

Page references to illustrations are printed in *italic* type

Abalone 13, 32; *13, 112*
Above-People 77
Acweeks 36
Agricultural programme 20
Alaska 7, 11, 13
Alert Bay 67
Amhalayt *83*
Amulets 76
Ancestors 37, 38, 73; *39, 122*
Animal: marriages 99–100; myths 97–8; spirits 70, 72–3
Armour 13, 67
Arrow chain 90, 97
Art styles 12–13, 105–6
Asia 10
Athabascan 12, 13, 59

Baby-Minders 106
Band 20, 22
Band council 22
Barrenness 66
Basketwork *34*

Bathing 33
Baxbakualanuxsiwae 70, 113, 114; *see also* Cannibal-at-the-North-End-of-the-World
Beaches 27
Bear 70, 73, 95, 99; *29, 34, 41, 42, 65, 66*
Bear Dancer 118
Bear-Husband 99–100
Bear-Mother *28*
Bear's grease 33
Beaver *26, 48, 61, 118*
Bella Bella 11, 104, 120; *see also* Kwakiutl
Bella Coola 11, 97, 120
Bering Straits 10
Berry patches 32
Big-House 27
Blankets and robes 18, 32, 34, 41, 51, 65; *33, 45, 70, 84, 108, 109;* copper purchase 59–60; currency 66; distribution of 52; Hudson's Bay 48, 66; payment to shaman 78
Bluejay 92, 95, 97

Boas, Franz 12
Body painting 33
Bokwus 96
Bone game 30
Box drum 78; *105*
Boxes 13, 29, 41, 75; *12, 54, 72, 85*
Bracelets 34
Bride-price 42–6
British Columbia 7, 9
British Columbia Homemakers 22
British Sovereignty 18
Burning prairies 97
Button blankets 59; *45*

Caduveo 12
Cannibal 110; cry 113; Dancer 110, 120; at-the-North-End-of-the-World 97 (*see also* Baxbakualanuxsiwae); pole 115; song 115, 116; spirit 65
Cannibalism 116
Canoe-People 77
Canoes 13, 25–7, 31; burial

97; ceremonial 52; dish *32*; prow ornaments *24, 53*; symbolic 113; song 52; used in potlatch 57
Cape Flattery 12
Carving 28, 29–30, 41, 104–5
Canton (China) 17
Cedar bark rings 61, 113
Ceremonial: Bella Coola 120; Kwakiutl 112–16; Nootka 122–4; Salish 106–110; Tlingit 118–120; Tsimshian 120
Ceremonial Days 55
Charms 76; shamanistic 78, 83; *76, 77, 81*
Chief-Above 89
Chief of the Dead 96
Chiefs 36, 41, 48, 64–5; robe *109*; staff *113*
Chilkat 32; weaving *34, 108; see also* Tlingit
China 13; Chinese 12; *17*
Chinook 13
Christianity 18–19
Chukchee 12
Clan 37, 47, 100; divisions

37; hats 61; *12, 37, 50*;
myths 37, 38–41, 100–101
Climate 9
Clothing 34, 41;
  ceremonial 34, 52–3, 104; *45*
Clover fields 32
Clowns 122
Clubs, ceremonial 58, *122–3*
Coast Range 7
Coast Salish *see* Salish
Columbia River 7, 13
Commemorative carving
  86, *87*
Commoners 41, 42, 46, 52
Compulsive magic 76
Concubines 46
Cook, Capt. James 13–17,
  25; *Journal* 13
Copper, source 59;
  headdress *102–3*; used in
  masks *105*; *60*
Coppers 45–6, 59–60; *61*;
  section *61*
Cormorant 95
Corpse 32, 114, 116; mask *98*
Cosmetics 34
Cradles *46*
Crane, shamanistic *104*
Cranmer, Daniel 67
Creation myth 89
Creator 89
Credit system 48
Cremation 62
Crest 38–41, 73, 120;
  headdress *93*; helmet
  124; post *27*
Crooked-Beak-of-Heaven 66
Crow 95, 100
Crown, shaman's *79*
Crown Property 20
Curing, shamanistic 78–81;
  song 80

Dalles, the 13
Dance 19; *see also*
  Ceremonial
Dancers 52–53, *103*;
  attendants *109*;
  insignia *108*
Dancers Society 120
Dance Spirit 106
Dancing Societies 104,
  110–16
Dead souls 97
Death, nature of 95–7
Deer 98
Dentalia shell 32; *43*
Devilfish, shamanistic *70*
Disease objects 78, 81
Diseases 18; *see also*
  Smallpox
Dish, ceremonial 57; *57*
Divorce 47
Dixon, Captain 17
Dluwulaxa Society 110,
  116–17
Dog, killed at grave 86;
  ritually devoured 118
Dog-Eaters' Society 111,
  118, 120
Dog-Fish 46, 99, *102–3, 114*
Dog-Fish-People *99*
Dog-Husband 99, 100

Double-Headed Eagle *45*
Double-Headed Monster 77
Double-Headed Serpent 70,
  75, 121–2
Douglas, Governor 18, 20
Dramatizations of Dreams 106
Dreams 83; *see also* Trances
Dried salmon 13, 31
Drums 106; *105*; drummers
  108–9; drumming 30, 123
Dual image *11, 57, 76*

Eagle *90*; *37, 40, 57, 111,
  124*; clan division 37
Eagle Dancer 53
Eagle down 81
Eating contests 57
Economy 10, 11, 18, 31–2
Edenshaw, Charles *46*
Education 20
Ehetisat (Nootka) 37
Ermine 97
Eroticism 95; *11*
Eulachon 32
European, in carving *18*;
  concepts 22; explorers 11,
  13–17, 25; *see also*
  Traders, European
Face-painting 33, 70, 76,
  108, 120
False marriages 42
Family, Indian 22; history
  38, 41, 55–7; *44*;
  organization 36
Fasting 75
Feasts 18, 27, 31, 32, 41, 48, 57
Feuds 48, 54, 67
Fire 77
Fireplaces 28
Fire-Thrower 116, 117
First Salmon Rite 31, 70
Fishing 22, 31; fishing
  localities 48
Fish-Eaters 31
Fish hook 41; *31*
Fish oil 13, 30, 32, 57–9, 66
Flood stories 99
Flying Frog *101*
Food dishes *14, 32, 56, 57*
Food storage 30
Fool-Dancer 116
Forehead mask *see* Frontlet
Forest-People 77
Forests 9
Fraser River stonework 9, 11
Frog 38–41, 95; *41, 101*
Frog-People 38
Frontlet 118; *118*
Fur trade *see* Traders,
  European

Ga-git *71*
Gambling 30; sticks *77*
Geography of area 7–9
Ghost Dancers 113
Ghosts 95
Giant shark 70
Giant squid 70
Gitskan (Tsimshian) 11
Gonakadet (sea monster) 70
Graves 86; grave boxes 95; *85*
Grizzly Bear Dancer 116;
  Cannibal 52

Grease feast 57
Grouse 56
Guaicuru 12
Guardian spirits 106, 120

Haida 11, 25, 28, 33, 37, 41,
  43, 64, 92, 99, 104, 106,
  118, 120; shaman 77
Haidzemerhs, Chief 39
Hamatsa 110, 112–16, 117
Hamshamtses 116
Harpoon whaling 32
Harrison, Charles
  (missionary) 25
Hawk *88, 117*
Head-flattening 34
Healing-Dancer 117
Heart, wooden *97*
Heiltsuk *see* Bella Bella,
  Kwakiutl
Hero tales 101
Hole-Through-the-Sky *39*
House in the Sky 89
House of the Original-
  People 90
House of the Wolves 122
House posts 27, 38, 44; *28,
  39, 48, 125*
Households 36–7
Houses 10, 27–8;
  ceremonial 30, 104, 113;
  interior *36*; ritual
  significance 30
Hoxhok *105*
Hudson's Bay Company 17
Hunting 32; rituals 70

Ice 101
Ice-Age 7, 10
Illness, curing 78–81
Indian Act 19–20, 60, 67
Indian Agents 20
Indian Dancing 110
Indian prophets 18
Indian status 20
Infidelity 47
Inheritance 41, 47; by
  women 42; of wife 46
Initiation 111–12; *see also*
  Ceremonial
Insult song 54–5, 58
Interest on loans 48

Japan Current 9, 31
Jewitt, John 28, 41
Joy Feasts 62
Juan de Fuca Strait 12

Kaigani Haida 11, 120
Killer Whale 38, 98; *27, 82,
  105*; clan division 37
Killer Whale Dancer 120
King, James 14, 25
Kinqalalala 114–15
Kinship 37
Knight Inlet 11
Koryak 12
Kwakiutl 11, 28, 29, 34, 37,
  42, 45, 46, 48, 52, 60, 62,
  65, 67, 70, 73, 87, 97,
  104, 106, 120; shamans 78
Kwakwabalas 78

Labret 34
Ladder-to-the-Sky 97
Lagius, Chief 45
Land-of-the-Dead 83, 97, 113
Land-of-the-Forever-Dead 83
Land Otter 73, 77
Language groups 11–12;
  division 99
Laughing competitions 30
Lazy-Boy 101
Lévi-Strauss, Claude 12
Lightnings 75
Ligi-ralwil *39*
Loans 48
Logging 22; camps 18
Longhouse 27
Loqwana (Wolf Dance) 122
Love charms 46
Lower-World 87

Magic 76, 78, 85, 98, 111
Magic Wooden Hat 99
Makah (Nootka) 12
Maori 12
Maquinna 28, 42
Marriage 42–6, 65, 112;
  Indian/White 20; with
  animals (myth) 99–100
Masks 18, 34, 67, 104–5
Massage 81
Medicine Spirits 106
Memorial poles 38, 64
Memorial potlatch 62
Mica 75
Milbanke Sound 11
Mink 90, 92, 95
Mission schools 20
Missionaries 18–19, 81
Mitla 120
Moachat (Nootka) 37
Monsters 70; bird *66*;
  crest *49, 83*
Moon 90; mask *117*
Mosquito 97; mask *114*
Moss 9; *8*
Mountain Goat 97; *12*
Mountain goat horn spoon *59*
Mountain sheep horn bowl *56*
Mourning Feasts 62
Mouth-at-Each-End 95
Murder 87

Nahen *29*
Names 42, 48, 51, 54, 57,
  110; house 30
Naming-to-Death 84
Nass River 7, 11
Natcitlaneh 38
Native Brotherhood 22
Native rights 22
Natural resources 10
Navigation 10
Niska (Tsimshian) 11
Nobles 41, 42, 46–7, 52
Nontsistalal 116
Nootka 11, 25, 28, 30, 32,
  33, 37, 43, 64, 70, 84–5,
  98, 99, 104, 105; dances
  122–4; shaman 83
Nootka Sound 13
North West Fur Company 17
Northwest Passage 13
North Wind 101

Nose-like-Coho 49
Nulmal 116; *116, 122*
Nutlam 111, 117
Ocean-People 77
Octopus, shamanistic 70
Oil dish 32, 56
Oil feast 57–9
Old Men 112
Original-People 90, 97, 99
Origin tales 89–92, 122
Ornaments 34, 41; *13, 43, 112, 115*
Other World 83
Otter 90
Owl 73, 97; *24, 97*
Owl-Man 86
Ownership 14, 30, 32, 47
Oyster-Catcher *33*

Paint brush *47*
Partition screen 28, 54; *29*
Patshatl 51
Pattern board *34*
Perez, Juan 13
Periwinkle 98
Petroglyphs (rock-carvings) *19*, 68–9
Physical appearance 12
Pictographs *see* Petroglyphs
Pile-driver *13*
Place-of-Opening *39*
Place-of-Supernatural-Power *113*
Planking 27, 28, 31
Pleistocene glaciation 7
Polygamy 46
Population 11, 18, 22
Porcupine 98
Porcupine quillwork 13; *84*
Porpoise 90
Porpoise-Woman 90
Portrait masks *15, 16, 18, 35, 106–7, 119, 120, 121*
Potlatch 17, 18, 48, 51–66, 67, 116
Power ceremony 120; name 120; stick 106
Prayer: to Halibut 72; to Salmon 72; to Trees 87
Prehistory 10, 11–13
Prince of Wales Island 11
Prince Rupert 9, 11
Privilege 38, 47–8, 51, 67, 69, 115
Property: destruction and distribution 59; ownership 38, 47–8, 67;
Prostitution 18, 19
Puget Sound 11, 13
Puppet *78*
Purification rites 116, 124

Quartz, supernatural 70
Quatsino Sound 122
Queen Charlotte Islands 10, 11, 13, 25; *8, 23, 94–5, 125*
Quileute (Salish) 90

Rainbow 92, 97
Rain Coast *8*
Rank 41; *see also* Status
Ransom 42
Rattles 78; *72–3, 79, 82*

Raven 90, 92–5, 97, 99; *59, 94–5*; clan division 37; house entrance 38
Raven Dancer 118
Registered Indians 20
Reincarnation 73, 83, 87, 99; animals 31, 70
Religion 101, 103
Reservations 20, 22
Retirement of dancer 112
Riou, Edward 17
Ritual 70–72; shamanistic 85
Ritual bathing 75–6
Rivers Inlet 11
Robin 98
Russians 13

Salish 11, 28, 37, 46, 47, 62, 64–5, 70, 73, 83, 87, 90, 98, 99, 104; shaman 77, 78; Spirit Singing 106–10
Salmon 31, 99; *31, 72–3*
Salmon-Home-beneath-the-Sea 31
Samwell, David 84
Sanctions against household members 37–8
Schools 20, 22
Scramble 65
Sea Lion 38, 95
Sea-monsters *93*
Sea otter 17, 31; *14*
Sea spirits 83
Seal 70, 95; *18*; mask 74–5
Seal Society 113, *114*
Seating, ceremonial 54, 110
Secret Societies 52; *see also* Dancing Societies
Secret songs 114
Self-Destroying Spirit 120
Settees *29; 30*
Shakayet *102–3*
Shakes, Chief 42; *29, 105*
Shaman 69, 70, 97, 104, 106; *79, 87*; apron *84*; charm *76*; dance wand *104*; grave box *85*; insignia 77; rattle *79, 82*; robe *70*; staff *79*
Shamanism 76–86
Shamanistic spirits 76, 77, 78, 83; *85*
Shamans' Society 110, 112, 120
Shell middens 32
Shrines 32
Siberians 12
Sisiutl 75, 121–2
Skate (fish) *33*
Skedans (Haida) *23*
Skeena River 7, 11; *90–91*
Skidegate (Haida) 99; *26*
Skil hats 64
Skulls, carved *115*; mask 98
Sky-Chief 94
Sky-World 90, 94, 97
Slave-Killer club 59; *58*
Slaves 28, 41–2, 59, 62
Smallpox 81, 106
Snail 90
Social groups 36–7
Social status *see* Status
Sorcerers and sorcery 69, 78, 86–7

Soul, symbolic 83
Soul-Catcher 83; *81*
Soul loss 81–3
Sparrow Society 112
Speaker 112; staff *113*
Speeches 43, 54–5, 58, 60
Spider-Woman 97
Spindle whorls *11, 36, 52*
Spirit possession 75, 83, 103, 106, 107–9, 116
Spirit Quest 75–6, 106
Spirits 31, 69–77, 78, 83, 87, 118, 122; acquisition 106; canoe 83; shaman *104*; songs 108, 113
Spirit Singing 104, 106–10
Split-Bear *39*
Split-Corpse 49
Split representation 12–13
Staff, ceremonial 112–3; *113*
Star 90
Status 17, 22, 41, 42, 47, 48, 51, 75, 117; of shaman 83
Stek-ya-den *10*
Stikine River 7
Stone-Ribs 101
Stonework 11; *9, 11, 13, 18, 62, 62–3*
Story-telling 30, 89, 101
Strait of Georgia 11
Sun 90, 94, 97; mask 117; *93, 111, 117*; woman who married the sun 97; tests son-in-law 101
Supernatural 38, 89; *see also* Spirits
Supernatural Season 103, 110

Tabus 110, 115–6, 122
Talking Stick *113*
Tattooing 34, 41
Tekijek *70*
Temlaxam *10, 90–91*
Tertiary glaciation 7
Theatre 111
Those-Who-Descend-from-the-Heavens *see* Dluwulaxa
Thrush 99
Thunderbird 75, 77; *52, 73*
Thunderstorms 75
Tides 9
Tide-Woman 99
Time of Tabu *see* Supernatural Season
Title to land 20, 22
Titles 66; *see also* Names
Tlingit 11, 37, 38, 45, 59, 61, 70, 92, 99, 104, 105, 118; dances 118–20; shaman 76
Tobacco mortar *9*
Tokens, of spirit-power 76
Torchlights *55*
Totem poles 10, 27, 38, 64; *26, 28, 39, 40, 41, 48, 49, 64, 65, 71, 100, 125*
Totems and totemism 38–41, 69, 73–5, 104; *31*
Toxwid 120–22
Trade 11, 13–17, 18, 47, 59, 66, 67, 104; trade beads *43*; goods 32; *12*

Traders, European 17, 18, 28
Trances 70, 75, 76, 104, 106; shamanistic 78
Transformation mask *101*
Transformation of the world 92
Transformation stories 90
Treaties 20, 22
Tribal boundaries 14, 48
Tribes 11–12
Trickster tales 92–7
Tsetseka 110
Tsimshian 11, 37, 38, 42, 59, 64, 86, 87, 92, 95, 104, 105, 118; dances 120
Tsonoqa 70
Twins, shamanistic powers 87

Union of British Columbia Chiefs 22
Utility boats 25, 27

Vancouver 9
Vancouver Island 7, 11, 12, 13, 18, 20
Venereal disease 18
Victoria 9, 18
Village Island 67
Villages 11, 25, 27, 30, 31, 32
Volcano-Woman 100
Vomiting, ritual function 66
Vomitor, carving 57

War 48, 67, 117; canoe *53*; club *67*; season 67; shaman's role 84–5
War Spirit 116, 117, 120
Washington State 7, 11
Watchmen 64
Water Monsters 70
Water Spirits 109; *70*
Wealth 17, 22, 47, 66; goods 17, 32
Weapons 41, 47; *42, 66, 67, 95*
Webber, John 33
Weirs 31
Welcoming Figure 104
Whale 31–2, 70, 90; *18, 57*
Whaling rituals 32
Whirlpool 101
Whisky 18
Whistles 110, 113, 120, 124
Wild-Man-of-the-Woods 96
Wild-Woman-of-the-Woods 70
Williwaws 9
Winter Ceremonial 101, 103–25
Witch Spirit *104*
Wolf 73, 98, 99, 111, 118, 122; *39, 50*; clan division 37; mask 122; *118*
Wolf Dance 99, 104, 122–4
Women's dances 109
Wren 90, 95

Xwé Xwé, mask *105*

Yakutat Bay 7
Yaqalenala 56
Yukaghir 12

OC